Sewing for Fashion Design

Sewing for Fashion Design

NURIE RELIS   and   GAIL STRAUSS
FASHION INSTITUTE OF TECHNOLOGY
New York, New York

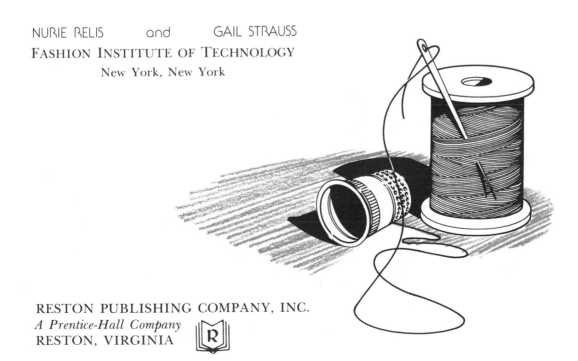

RESTON PUBLISHING COMPANY, INC.
A Prentice-Hall Company
RESTON, VIRGINIA

LIBRARY OF CONGRESS CATALOGING IN
PUBLICATION DATA

Relis, Nurie
  Sewing for fashion design.

  Includes index.
  1. Sewing. 2. Machine sewing. I. Strauss, Gail,
joint author. II. Title.
TT715.R44   646.4'04   78-8557
ISBN 0-87909-755-8

© 1978 by Reston Publishing Company, Inc.
A Prentice-Hall Company
Reston, Virginia 22090

10   9   8   7   6   5   4   3

Printed in the United States of America

to our students, who have been an inspiration for this book

Contents

Preface

This book is an outgrowth of Seventh Avenue sewing procedures that have been taught in the Design Room Techniques course at the Fashion Institute of Technology.

It is with deep appreciation that we wish to express our thanks to those who were helpful in very many ways: Professor Dorothy Hannenberg of F.I.T., who opened doors on Seventh Avenue, and the following people in the industry who were generous in giving us their time and information. Bill Tice of Malcolm Star, who put us in the capable hands of Anna Trevison; Ted Falino of Jerry Silverman; Donald Hopson of Kasper for Joan Leslie, who introduced us to Sally O'Kanto and Antonio Grassi; Terry

O'Neil of Bill Blass, Inc., who introduced us to Henry Bialowas; Lee Lo Cascio of Manhattan Scalloping; Professor Hilde Jaffe, chairperson of the Fashion Design department of F.I.T., for her valuable feedback during the formation and presentation of the material; Rosemary E. Celandine for the care with which she read the manuscript and made necessary corrections; Rochelle B. Fink for the typing of the manuscript; Rita Hirsch for her assistance in the presentation of the manuscript; the editors and staff who were eager to have us write this book, while recognizing the audience for which it was intended.

We would also like to express our gratitude to the following companies: Armo Company division of Crown Textiles Manufacturing Corporation; Belding Corticelli Company; Coats and Clark Company; Dan River Fabrics, Inc.; Donahue Sales; Pellon Corporation; Singer Sewing Machine Company; and Stacy Fabrics.

NURIE RELIS
GAIL STRAUSS

Sewing for Fashion Design

1
Use of Materials

INTRODUCTION

On Seventh Avenue one sees how fashion history, methods, and ideas have influenced and shaped the world of fashion. The successful fashion designer has a thorough knowledge of sketching, draping, patternmaking, and sewing. Sample hands, through years of experience, have developed the technical expertise and craftsmanship necessary to create thoroughly professional garments.

This book is an in-depth study of the sewing techniques of quality dress and sportswear firms that can be used to refine previous knowledge of sewing. This is the type of sewing that will enable the student of fashion design to develop the technical expertise and craftsmanship necessary to create a garment with the professional touch.

Each section provides step-by-step instructions, illustrated by corresponding sketches, to describe clearly the various aspects of sample room sewing. In addition, the reference materials on tools, fabrics, and stitching supply information important to the development of successful garments.

EQUIPMENT

The well-run sample room is equipped with one or two large cutting tables, several lock-stitch power sewing machines, pressing equipment, dress forms, mirrors, a rack for garments, and the following tools.

Sewing Tools

HAND SEWING NEEDLES: sized from coarse (#1) to very fine (#10). Sharps are medium needles used for permanent hand stitching. Milliner's are longer and most frequently used for bastings. Ballpoint needles are used to sew fine knits (tricots). Glovers needles are used to stitch leather, synthetic suede, vinyl, and furs.

SEWING MACHINE NEEDLES: sized fine to heavy. They should conform to the weight and type of fabric used. Ballpoint needles permit ease in stitching knits. Machine wedge needles are necessary for leather, synthetic suede, and vinyl.

PINS: satin steel pins recommended. Number 17 will usually do for most fabrics, number 14 for fine fabrics, and ballpoint pins for fine knits.

THIMBLES: an aid to efficient hand sewing. An acceptable thimble is metal and fits snugly on the middle finger of the needle-holding hand. There are two types of thimbles: the tailor's thimble, which is open at the top, and the dressmaker's thimble, which is closed.

needles

thimbles

pins

SEWING TOOLS

BEESWAX: used to coat thread for easier threading.

Cutting Tools

All types of shears and scissors are available for both the right and the left hand.

BENT-HANDLE DRESSMAKER SHEARS: 8 to 10 inches long, for cutting fabric. Scissors 5 or 6 inches long are used for light cutting, trimming, and clipping corners and curves.

THREAD CLIPPERS: an efficient tool for clipping threads for both hand and machine sewing, they can also be used in clipping curves and opening buttonholes.

PINKING SHEARS: 9 or 10 inches long, used to give a zig-zag finish to raw edges of firmly woven fabrics.

SEAM RIPPER: for ripping out unnecessary stitches and for opening machine-stitched buttonholes.

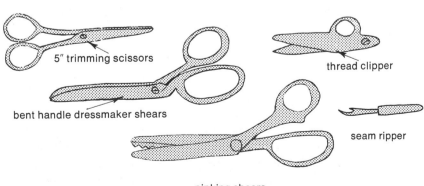

5″ trimming scissors

thread clipper

bent handle dressmaker shears

seam ripper

pinking shears

CUTTING TOOLS

Measuring Tools

TAPE MEASURE: smooth-surfaced, clearly marked with centimeters as well as the familiar inches.

RULER: clear plastic, marked with both centimeters and inches—1 inch wide by 6 inches long and 2 inches wide by 18 inches long.

YARD STICK: available in 36- or 45-inch lengths, made out of metal or wood.

SKIRT MARKER: for marking hem lengths accurately. Markers are available for use with chalk or pins.

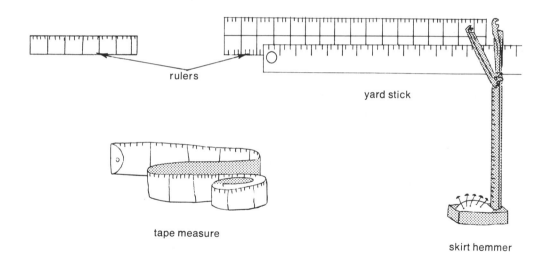

rulers

yard stick

tape measure

skirt hemmer

Marking Tools

tracing wheel

TRACING WHEEL: used to transfer pattern markings to fabric with tracing paper. The small serrated-edge tracing wheel is used for most fabrics. To avoid snagging, a smooth-edge tracing wheel is recommended for fine and knit fabrics.

TRACING PAPER: carbon-coated paper used in conjunction with the tracing wheel for transferring pattern markings to fabrics. White tracing paper should be used on fabric.

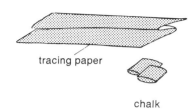

tracing paper

chalk

GRAPHITE PAPER: colored coated graphite paper, available in art supply stores, used where carbon would not be visible.

TAILOR'S CHALK: may be made of wax or stone. It is used to transfer marking to fabrics that will not accommodate carbon paper, and can also be used for marking adjustments in fittings and for hems. Wax chalk is advisable for woolens; for all other fabrics use stone chalk or chalk marking pencils.

Sewing Machine Attachments

CORDING FOOT: left- and right-handed. Use of either permits even, close stitching for cording and zippers.

PIPING FOOT: for finishing bias binding strips.

GATHERING FOOT: for even, permanent shirring.

ROLLER FOOT: good for stitching on leather, synthetic suede, and vinyl.

INVISIBLE ZIPPER FOOT: for stitching the invisible zipper.

NARROW HEMMER FOOT: for rolled machine hem stitching.

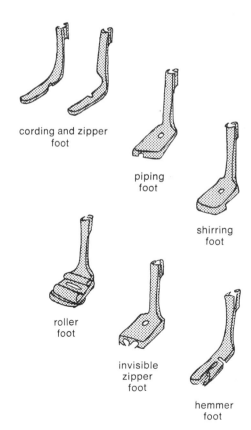

cording and zipper foot

piping foot

shirring foot

roller foot

invisible zipper foot

hemmer foot

Miscellaneous Tools

LOOP TURNER: used for turning bias strips to make "spaghetti" cord and narrow belts.

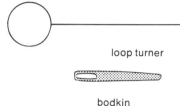

loop turner

bodkin

BODKIN: used for threading ribbon and elastic through a tunnel or casing.

DRESS FORM: a professional dress form on an adjustable stand. Collapsible shoulders have a distinct advantage for fitting any type of garment.

Pressing Equipment

The difference between professional and nonprofessional results in sewing often depends on proper pressing technique and the pressing equipment available.

STEAM AND DRY IRON: a heavy iron with adjustable temperature controls.

IRONING BOARD: a well-padded shaped board, which stands firmly on the floor.

SLEEVE BOARD: a well-padded miniature board useful for pressing sleeves and small areas.

SEAM ROLL: a padded roll for pressing hard-to-reach seams. Its use will prevent imprints when seams are pressed open.

TAILOR'S HAM: used for pressing and molding curved areas.

TAILOR BOARD OR POINT PRESSER: an unpadded device helpful for pressing points.

NEEDLE OR VELVET BOARD: necessary for pressing velvet, velveteen, and napped and fur fabrics.

PRESS MITT: used on the hand to press small areas without interfering with the rest of the garment.

PRESS CLOTH: firmly woven drill cotton and wool cloths, necessary to protect fabrics from shine or scorching when pressing on the right side of the garment. A large piece of velour wool is necessary to cover the ironing board surface when pressing synthetic suede.

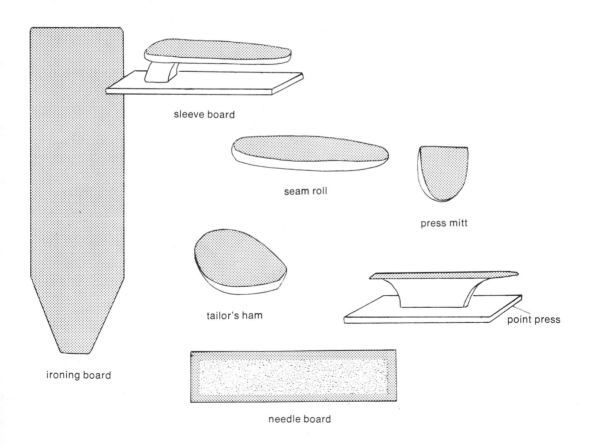

sleeve board

seam roll

press mitt

tailor's ham

point press

ironing board

needle board

PRESSING EQUIPMENT

Sewing Machines

The sample room is equipped with industrial power machines: there are lock stitch, overlock, and zigzag machines. The power machine is run by a foot treadle and uses a knee lift to raise and lower the presser foot. The overlock machine uses a foot pedal to raise and lower the presser foot.

THE LOCK STITCH MACHINE. The lock stitch machine is used for straight stitching. The presser foot can be adjusted for the type fabric that is used. Light pressure is needed for lightweight fabrics and increased pressure is necessary for heavier weights. The tension is always adjusted along with the presser foot for a strong secure stitch. The stitch length varies depending on the fabric. Seams are usually stitched with 12 to 14 stitches per inch.

Easing and gathering is done with about 8 to 12 stitches per inch. Stay stitching is done with 14 to 18 stitches per inch. A special attachment can be used for gathering: the size of the stitch will determine how much fabric is being gathered. Long stitches will gather more fabric than shorter stitches.

THE ZIGZAG MACHINE. The primary use of the zigzag machine is to applique lace, attach elastic, and provide a decorative finish for the edges of tricot knits. The zigzag stitch allows the fabric to stretch after the stitching is completed. The length of the zigzag is determined by the stitch size, and the width is set by a dial—the higher the number, the wider the stitches.

THE OVERLOCK MACHINE. The overlock machine combines straight and overcasting stitches and cuts and sews the fabric while stitching the seams. It has an elaborate threading process that uses three spools of thread. A sharp blade trims the fabric before the stitching operation. The finished seam produced by this machine is ideal for stretch and knit fabrics and the finished seam is ⅛ to ⅜ inch wide, depending on the machine setting.

THE SAFETY STITCH OVERLOCK MACHINE. The safety stitch overlock machine makes an additional row of stitching and uses 4 spools of thread. It is used for woven fabrics and makes seams that are ⅜ to ½ inch wide.

TEMPORARY STITCHING

Temporary stitching, unlike permanent stitching, should be removed as the garment is constructed. The stitches are generally larger and further apart than permanent stitches. Nylon, silk, or other thread with a continuous filament should be used, so that traces of the thread will not remain in the garment. Temporary thread should contrast slightly in color with the fabric.

Thread Tracing

A combination of long and short stitches is helpful for marking seams, centers, construction details, and crossmarks so that they are visible on the right side of

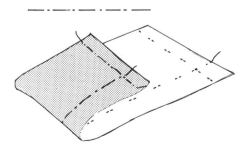

Thread Tracing

the fabric. The stitches follow the carbon or chalk lines copied on to the wrong side of the fabric from the original pattern. To facilitate easy removal, knots are not used. All corners are carefully intersected so that a cross is visible on the right side of the fabric. Crossmarks are made with a tiny running stitch.

Even Basting

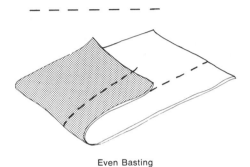

Even Basting

The most commonly used basting is a series of even stitches with a ⅜-inch pickup, used to join two or more layers of fabric. Use of this stitch permits accurate fitting and joining. Stitches are made a fraction of an inch inside the seam line in the seam allowance to prevent marking the right side of the garment and to allow machine stitching on the original seam line.

Uneven Basting

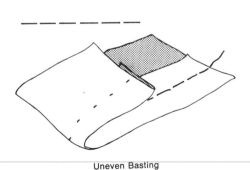

Uneven Basting

A combination of long and short stitches with the short stitch visible on the right side, uneven basting is used primarily to hold up the turned edge of hems and the finished edges of necklines and collars, as an aid in pressing the garment.

This method of stitching is used instead of thread tracing for curved areas.

Slip Basting

Slip basting on the right side is used when parts of a garment have been fitted and basting is necessary before they can be removed from the dress form (sleeves, waist, and skirt joinings are handled in this manner). Slip basting is also used in matching plaids, stripes, and prints; in this case, it is most efficient to baste from the right side of the fabric.

Slip the needle through the fold for ¼ inch and then through the seam line on the other side for ¼ inch. Return the needle through the fold and continue basting.

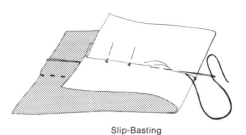
Slip-Basting

Machine Basting

Machine basting is a quick method for the temporary joining of two pieces of fabric. Use the largest size machine stitch. This method should not be used if alterations in the fit of the garment must be made later, and care should always be taken so that when the basting is removed, no evidence of thread residue or needle holes remains; garments should never be pressed with machine basting in place, because a lasting impression will result. Remove machine basting by snipping the top thread at frequent intervals and pulling out the bobbin thread first.

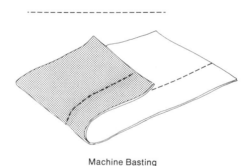
Machine Basting

Pin Basting

Pin basting is often used in the sample room to join pieces of a garment where fitting is unnecessary. Pins are placed along the seam line so that they can be easily removed during the stitching.

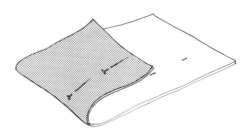
Pin Basting

Hand stitches are used where permanent stitches are necessary but machine stitching is not desirable. The stitch used depends on the garment styling, the fabric, and the area where the stitching is necessary. A single strand of matching thread is recommended for hand stitching.

Plain Hem Stitch

The hemming method most frequently utilized in the sample room is the plain hem stitch. This stitch is invisible on the right side of the garment and therefore is preferred for light and medium weight woven fabrics. When pressed, this stitch will not leave any impression on the right side. The folded edge of the hem or binding is used with this finish.

Pick up one thread of the fabric in the garment and insert the needle diagonally into the folded edge of the hem. Space the stitches ⅜ to ½ inch apart. To secure hand-finished waistbands, tailored buttonhole facings, and bindings, use a variation of this hem stitch, picking up the machine stitches instead of the folded edge.

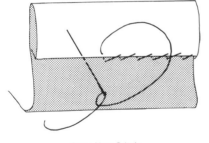

Plain Hem Stitch

Blind Hem Stitch

The blind hem stitch is used where the hem edge is held closely and stitches should show as little as possible on both the right and the wrong sides of the garment. The folded edge of the hem or binding may be used with this finish. Insert the needle into the edge of the hem, pick up one thread in the garment directly below the edge of the hem, slant the needle ⅜ inch away, and pick up the hem edge again. Slip the needle *through* the folded edge when hemming a sheer fabric.

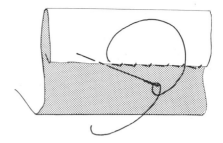

Blind Hem Stitch

Slip Hem Stitch

Though not the strongest of stitches, the slip hem is invisible on both right and wrong sides of the garment. When this hem is used on heavier fabrics, pressing will not leave the impression of the hem on the right side. For the slip hem, the raw edge is often finished by pinking. Fold back the edge of the hem ⅜ inch; pick up one thread of the hem, keeping the needle parallel to the edge; and then pick up one thread of the garment ⅜ inch away. The thread of the finished hem should have an even tension. If the edge is pinked and finished with a row of machine stitching, pick up the machine stitch.

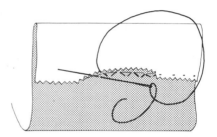

Slip Hem Stitch

Rolled Edge

A fine hand finish for chiffon, sheers, and lightweight silk is the rolled edge. To facilitate stitching the rolled hem, it is advisable to run a row of small machine stitches ¼ inch away from the raw edge and trim away ⅛ inch of the fabric. The edge of the fabric is rolled over the machine stitching to the wrong side and finished with a plain hem stitch.

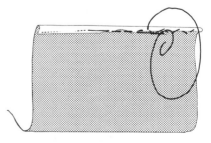

Rolled Edge

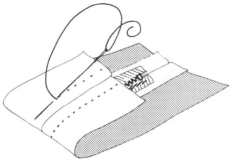

Pick Stitch

Pick Stitch

The pick stitch is a hand stitch for inserting zippers. Bring the needle up from the underside of the garment and then insert the needle back one or two threads through the layers of fabric and zipper. Space the stitches ¼ inch apart.

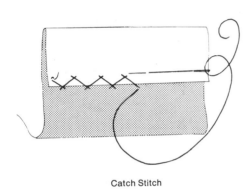

Catch Stitch

Catch Stitch

Because it allows for stretching, the catch stitch is used to hem knits, bias cuts, and loosely woven woolens and to attach interfacings and facings. This stitch is often used for lined garments where the raw edge is left unfinished. Working from left to right, pick up one thread close to the hem edge, and then cross over diagonally into the garment; another pickup ¼ inch away completes the cross-over stitch. In order to maintain the stretching effect of this stitch, the thread should not be pulled tightly.

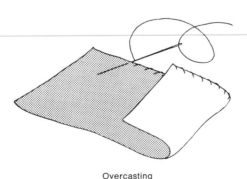

Overcasting

Overcasting

The overcast stitch is one choice for finishing the raveling edge of fabrics, although hand overcasting is not generally used in the sample room. To prevent the thread from tangling, stitch from right to left. In an over and over motion, pick up diagonal stitches ⅛ inch below the raw edge, spacing stitches ⅜ inch apart.

Back Stitching

Back stitches are small stitches that overlap on the underside and resemble machine stitching on the inside. The back stitch is used to secure pockets from the inside of the garment. Starting on the inside at the top of the pocket, take a stitch ⅛ inch long through the under layer of fabric. Take the needle back to the starting point and take another stitch, bringing the needle up ⅛ inch past the first stitch. Continue until the pocket is securely stitched into place.

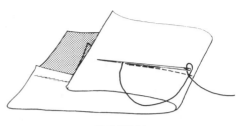

Back Stitching

Saddle Stitch

The saddle stitch is a fine decorative top stitch using buttonhole twist or embroidery floss in a matching or contrasting color. It may be a combination of long and short stitches, or even stitches, evenly spaced from the finished edge of the seam or garment.

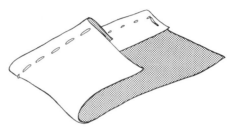

Saddle Stitch

Staystitching

Staystitching is a row of small machine stitches, through a single layer, used to prevent raveling, stretching, or curling of the fabric at neckline curves, corners, and points.

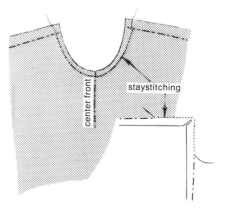

center front

staystitching

Staystitching

The method selected for finishing the raw edge of a seam depends upon the kind of fabric used, the type of garment (sportswear, children's wear, evening wear, etc.), and the need for a decorative touch. The primary purpose of a seam finish is the prevention of raveling, stretching, or curling. Sample room seam allowances are 1 inch for straight edges and ½ inch for curves. There are sample rooms, however, where an overall ½ inch seam allowance is used. In preparing the seam for the correct finish, the seam is stitched, trimmed when necessary, and pressed.

Trimming, Clipping, and Grading

When a garment has been fitted and approved, curved seam allowances are trimmed and clipped or notched where necessary to allow the seams to lie flat and smooth when pressed. A curved seam may be trimmed to ¼ inch, depending on the degree of curve.

To prevent ridge marks on the surface of the garment left by the seam allowance on straight or curved edges of necklines, collars, and cuffs, the seam allowance is graded by trimming it in layers. The layer of seam allowance closest to the surface of the garment is trimmed to ¼ inch and the other layer is trimmed to ⅛ inch. Interfacing is trimmed to the seam line.

After grading, curved edges are clipped or notched. Inward curves should be clipped to within ¹/₁₆ inch of the seam line at ½ inch intervals. Outward curves should be notched (triangular wedges) at ½ inch intervals to prevent the seam allowance from overlapping. When notching two layers of fabric, notch each layer alternately.

Tacking

When joining two layers of fabric together, the seam is secured by tacking at the start and the finish. To accomplish this on the industrial lock stitch machine, a few stitches are sewn and then, with both the needle and presser foot in the raised position, the fabric is brought forward and restitched. Repeat this procedure at the finish of the seam.

On machines that have an automatic reverse, tacking is accomplished by using the reverse lever for a few stitches at the start and at the finish of the seam.

Tailor's Knot

The tailor's knot is used as a substitute for machine tacking. When you have completed your stitching, cut the thread, leaving about 3 inches extending from the fabric. Holding the threads together, form a loop into a loose knot and slide the knot to the base of the thread where it emerges from the fabric. Pull the thread to tighten the knot. Cut away excess thread.

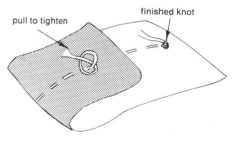

Tailor's Knot

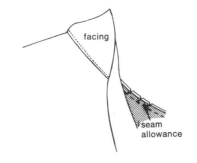

facing

seam
allowance

Back Stitching

Back Stitching

Back stitching is used to hold facings to the inside of the garment. After the seam has been stitched, trimmed, and graded, turn the facing to the inside and edge stitch along the seam line, attaching the facing to the seam allowance.

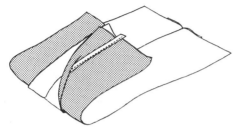

Taped Seam

Taped Seam

To prevent a seam from stretching, use a twill tape to support the seam. Place the tape in the seam allowance area of the garment and catch one edge of the tape while stitching.

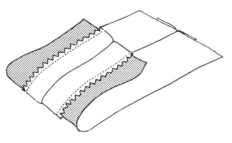

Stitched and Pinked Finish

Stitched and Pinked Seam

The stitched and pinked finish is generally used on firmly woven fabrics that do not ravel. Machine stitch ¼ inch from the raw edge and using pinking shears trim away excess fabric.

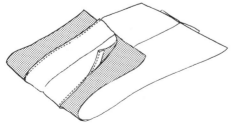

Edge Stitch

Edge Stitch

The edge stitch is a finish suitable for tightly woven light to medium weight fabrics. Turn under ¼ inch of the raw edge. With the raw edge facing up, machine stitch $1/32$ inch from the folded edge. To prevent stretching of curved or bias edges, a stay stitch ⅛ inch from the raw edge will be helpful.

French Seam

The French seam is a suitable finish for sheer fabrics when any other finish would be visible on the right side of the garment. The French seam finish is no more than ¼ inch; a ½ inch seam allowance is advisable. With wrong sides together, stitch ¼ inch from the raw edge and trim to ⅛ inch (if the fabric ravels, use two rows of stitching before trimming). Turn to the right side and crease along the stitching; then stitch ¼ inch from the creased edge.

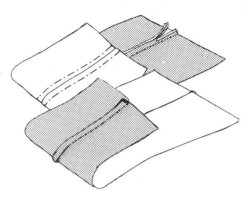

French Seam

Mock French Seam

Another finish for sheer fabrics is an imitation French seam. Stitch with a ¼ inch seam allowance. Trim away one thickness of fabric, leaving ⅛ inch. Fold the ¼ inch seam allowance over the ⅛ inch seam allowance, leaving ⅛ inch below the seam line; stitch just inside the original seam. Trim away the excess fabric at the seamline.

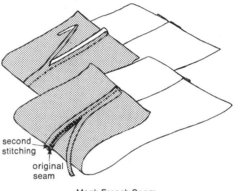

second stitching

original seam

Mock French Seam

Bound Seam

Bound seams are used to assure a clean finish for unlined jackets. To prepare bias binding, see the section on bias in Part 3.

For the couture finish, cut bias binding strips in chiffon or silk. Using 1-inch-wide bias strips, stitch, right sides together, ¼ inch away from the raw edges. Fold the bias strips, encasing the raw edges. Turn under the raw edge of the bias strip ¼ inch and plain hem, picking up the machine stitches.

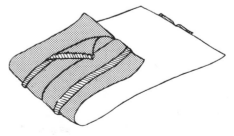

Bound Seam

In better sportswear, cotton or rayon bias binding is used. Use the binding attachment on the sewing machine to encase the raw edges of the fabric in bias strips.

Flat Fell Seam

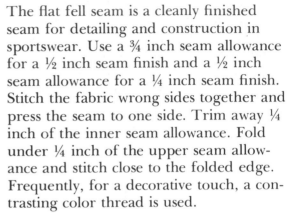

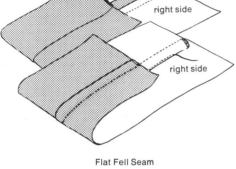

right side

right side

Flat Fell Seam

The flat fell seam is a cleanly finished seam for detailing and construction in sportswear. Use a ¾ inch seam allowance for a ½ inch seam finish and a ½ inch seam allowance for a ¼ inch seam finish. Stitch the fabric wrong sides together and press the seam to one side. Trim away ¼ inch of the inner seam allowance. Fold under ¼ inch of the upper seam allowance and stitch close to the folded edge. Frequently, for a decorative touch, a contrasting color thread is used.

Welt Seam

Welt Seam

The welt seam is a decorative finish for bulky fabrics. In appearance, the welt seam is similar to the wrong side of the flat fell seam. Join the fabric, right sides together, with the seam allowance. The width of the seam allowance used determines the width of the welt. Trim the inner seam allowance to ¼ inch. The final stitch, encasing the trimmed seam, creates the fullness of this finish.

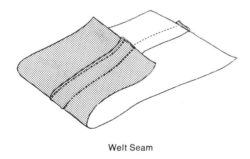

Lapped Seam

Lapped Seam

A top-stitched seam often used for yoke detailing is the lapped seam. Fold and press under the edge of the overlapped section. Pin the lapped edge to the right side along the seam line and stitch close to the fold. For a loose edge, stitch ¼ inch from the folded edge.

Slot Seam

The slot seam is a decorative seam. The width varies, depending on the area where the seam is desired. The seam is made with an underlay, which is cut to a width double that of the seam allowance. To prepare the seam for stitching, join right sides together and machine baste on the seam line. Press the seam open and carefully align the underlay before pinning the right sides together. On the right side, baste along the desired width for machine stitching. Remove the basting that closes the seam. For a decorative effect the color of the thread and the stitch size may vary; often a contrasting color is used for the underlay.

For curved slot seams, both sides of the seam must be faced, and the underlay follows the same curve.

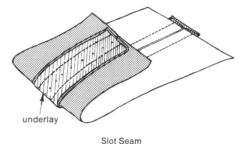

underlay

Slot Seam

Crack Stitch

A nearly invisible machine stitch, the crack stitch is stitched from the right side of the garment and is used to finish waistbands, cuffs, and bindings. After the waistband, cuff, or binding is attached to the garment, turn under the raw edge ¼ inch, fold the waistband, cuff, or binding to the wrong side and pin it ¼ inch beyond the stitching. Baste on the right side. Stitch in the seam "well" (the "well" is the joined seam line).

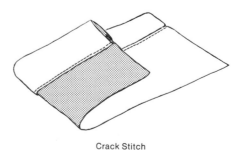

Crack Stitch

Hong Kong Finish

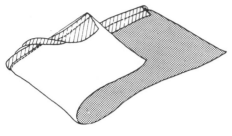

Hong Kong Finish

A couture finish on the hem edge, the Hong Kong finish takes a little extra time and requires superior workmanship. Use a bias strip cut 1 inch wide and place the garment and strip right sides together. Machine stitch ¼ inch from the raw edge. Turn the bias strip to the wrong side, encasing the raw edge, and finish with a crack stitch.

Pointed Seams

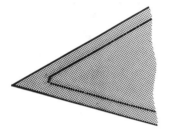

Pointed Seam

A pointed seam on collar, cuffs, or lapels, must be stitched blunt at the corners to achieve a well-formed point. On fine fabrics, take one stitch across at the point; on medium fabrics, take two stitches across at the point; and on heavy fabrics, take three stitches. Trim and turn to the right side, being careful not to stretch the point.

STITCHING GUIDE

The chart summarizes information on choosing the correct needles, thread, and number of stitches per inch. Always test with a sample of the fabric selected.

Needles

Hand or machine needles are determined by the selection of fabric. Use a fine needle with fine fabrics and heavier or coarser needles with heavier fabrics. The point should be sharp in order to penetrate the fabric easily.

Selection of Needles, Thread, and Number of Stitches per Inch

Fabric	Hand Needles	Machine Needles	Thread	Machine Stitches Per Inch
Lightweight	9, 10 Milliner's or Sharps	Fine 9-10 Ball-point 10-11	Mercerized Cotton Cotton and Polyester Silk	12-16
Medium Lightweight	8-9 Milliner's or Sharps	Fine 11-14 Medium Ball-point 10-12	Mercerized Cotton Cotton and Polyester Silk	12-14
Medium	7-8 Milliner's or Sharps	Medium 12-14 Ball-point 10-14	Mercerized Cotton Cotton and Polyester Silk	10-14
Medium Heavy	6 Milliner's or Sharps	Medium Coarse 14-16	Mercerized Cotton Cotton and Polyester Silk	10-12
Heavy-weight	1-5 Milliner's or Sharps	Coarse 16-20 Ball-point 16	Mercerized Cotton Cotton and Polyester Silk	8-12
Leather and Vinyl	Glovers	14 or 16 Wedge-point	Heavy-duty	6-10

Thread

Select the correct thread according to the fabric content. Thread size is indicated by numbers: the higher the number the finer the thread. Number 50 is medium weight. When letters are used instead of numbers, A is fine and D is heavy.

For temporary stitching, thread tracing, and basting, nylon silk or other thread with a continuous filament should be used, so that traces of the thread will not remain in the garment, and the color should contrast slightly (but not greatly) with the fabric. For superstitious reasons, green thread is never used for tracing or basting in the sample room.

For permanent stitching, select thread one shade darker than the fabric, because it will appear lighter after stitching. For hand sewing, cut the thread about 20 inches long to prevent tangling. Most hand sewing is done with a single strand of thread; a double strand is used for sewing on buttons, hooks and eyes, and snaps.

For hand-worked buttonholes, loops, and chains, use silk button twist, size D. Use this same thread for decorative top stitching, on the bobbin, as the top thread, or in both places, depending on the machine. The tension should be adjusted to accommodate the heavier thread.

Stitches per Inch

The number of stitches per inch is determined by the weight of the fabric. Fine fabric is usually stitched with short stitches and heavier fabric with longer stitches.

Textured fabrics use the longest stitch size recommended in each category.

In leather and suede, long stitches, making fewer needle holes, will prevent the fabric from ripping after stitching.

For top stitching, the length of the stitch is determined by the appearance desired and the weight of the fabric. Generally, top stitching requires long stitches. The tension and the pressure of the presser foot should be adjusted according to the thickness of the fabric.

Fabric Weights

This fabric classification is by weight only; the fiber content may be natural or manmade.

LIGHTWEIGHT: batiste, voile, cotton, organdy, chiffon, organza, lawn, silk surah.

MEDIUM LIGHTWEIGHT: challis, crepe, handerchief linen, taffeta, jersey.

MEDIUM WEIGHT: percale, polished cotton, madras, seersucker, velvet and velveteen, gingham, broadcloth, chambray, corduroy, shantung, chintz, pique, muslin, satin, double knits.

MEDIUM HEAVY: gabardine, twill, poplin, ticking, denim, flannel, linen, terry cloth, corduroy, velvet and velveteen.

HEAVY WEIGHT: fleece, camel's hair, canvas, duck, denim, hopsacking, synthetic suede, corduroy, sailcloth, velour, leather, vinyl.

Underlining

For a professional appearance, underlining is used in a garment to retain the shape and give support to the fabric. The choice of underlining fabric depends on the desired effect of the finished garment. To hold the garment shape but preserve a soft look, use a lightweight fabric. For a stiffer effect, use a fabric with more body.

China silk, chiffon, cotton batiste, marquisette, taffeta, and SiBonne are fabrics available for underlinings. For translucent fabrics, the color match of the underlining must be exact. The underlining must be compatible with the fabric for laundering or dry cleaning.

Interfacing

An interfacing is a layer of fabric placed between garment sections. The function of the interfacing is to give shape and support to such detail areas as collars, cuffs, pocket flaps, lapels, and waistbands. It also prevents stretching around the neckline, armholes, and pockets.

A variety of interfacings, known by trade names, include fabrics such as batiste, china silk, marquisette, organza, SiBonne, and siri, all of which may also be used for lining and backing of garments.

The choice of interfacing depends on the fabric texture and the design effect desired. Some garments may have a combination of different weights of interfacings. In areas that need interfacing to prevent stretching, choose an interfacing of a weight similar to or lighter than the fabric. In collars, the fabric should roll over the interfacing without forming sharp points and a hard edge. For collars, cuffs, lapels, waistband, and pocket details, the weight of the interfacing is determined by the degree of stiffness desired.

Most interfacings come in black or white. For use with sheer fabric, or where the interfacing shades through, the interfacing should match the color of the fabric as closely as possible.

Interfacing should be compatible with the garment fabric for dry cleaning and laundering.

Interfacing is available in several forms: woven, nonwoven, press-on, fusible, and fusible web are available in three weights: light, medium, and heavy.

WOVEN: This interfacing must be cut on grain if it is to behave compatibly with the fabric. Use the heaviest weight in tailored garments.

NONWOVEN: This type is generally best used where body and stiffness are desired. Some nonwoven interfacings have some bias stretch in their construction, which gives them a bit more flexibility.

PRESS-ON OR FUSIBLE WOVEN OR NON-WOVEN: This interfacing adheres to the fabric when applied with a hot iron. It is best used in small detail areas and must be tested for stiffness and ridge marks on the garment. After many washings or dry cleanings, there may be a loss of adhesion.

FUSIBLE WEB: The fusible web creates a press-on interfacing out of any fabric desired. It is especially useful for sheer fabrics when the sheerness is necessary for the appearance of the garment; organza or chiffon can be used to interface in this case. The web is placed between the sheer interfacing and the garment on the wrong side. When pressed with a heated iron, the two layers of fabric are joined. To separate, use steam and heat to loosen the web so that the two fabric layers can be pulled apart.

Lining

Lining a garment gives a neat finish to the inside and permits ease in slipping the garment on and off. In some instances, the lining helps give shape and support. The choice of fabric depends on the effect desired; use the same guidelines as for underlining. The lining must be compatible with the fabric for laundering or dry cleaning.

2
Preparation

PREPARATION OF WOVEN FABRICS

In order to assemble a garment following sample room procedure, an understanding of fabric is necessary.

Blocking the fabric insures the correct hang to a garment after it is constructed.

The fabric is torn or cut along the crosswise grain, so that the yarns at the raw edges can unravel. Tearing is faster, but may not be possible because of the nature of the weave. If necessary, pull a strand of yarn along the crosswise grain, and cut along this yarn.

If the selvage edge of the fabric is woven tightly and the fabric pulls, either remove the selvage by cutting along the lengthwise grain or clip through the selvage at 1-inch intervals.

selvage-lengthwise grain

crosswise grain

bias

lengthwise grain

Woven Fabric

If the yarns do not form a 90° angle, the fabric should be blocked. Fold the fabric to form a true bias, then stretch the entire length of the fabric, from selvage to selvage, pulling from the shorter end. Stretching on the true bias will line up the yarns squarely.

To set the yarns, press the fabric on the wrong side with the iron heated to the correct temperature.

Unfortunately, there are permanently finished fabrics that cannot be blocked into perfect alignment. It is best not to use these improperly finished fabrics for quality sewing. When these fabrics are used, however, one may ignore the grain and simply cut across the fabric at right angles to the selvage.

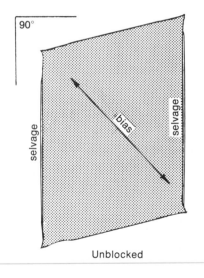

Unblocked

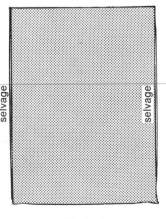

Blocked

LAYOUT AND CUTTING

Checklist for Pattern Pieces

1. Muslin pattern pieces, pressed

2. Lengthwise grainline marked on each pattern piece

3. Seam allowances trimmed evenly

4. Corresponding crossmarks indicated

5. Pieces to be laid along the fold separated from those to be cut double

Fabric Folds for Pattern Layout

The layout of pattern pieces on the fabric is planned for the least amount of waste.

On folded fabric, always plan the layout on the wrong side with the right sides together. The fabric may be folded along the lengthwise grain or the crosswise grain, or formed into a gate fold.

The number and width of the pattern pieces determines the direction in which the fabric is folded. Sometimes a combination of folds is necessary for the most economical layout.

Asymmetric and bias-cut patterns, or uneven plaids and stripes, should be cut unfolded. The layout is then planned on the right side of the fabric.

To fold the fabric along the *lengthwise grain,* fold the fabric in half and align the selvages. When the fabric is folded in this manner, the pattern pieces that are to be cut double should be laid with the grainline parallel to the selvage, and those that are to be cut in one piece should be positioned exactly on the fold. Smaller

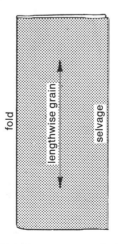

Fold On Lengthwise Grain

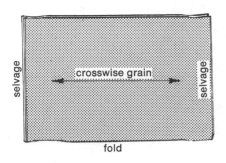

Fold On Crosswise Grain

pieces are interlocked into the layout for an economical use of the fabric. To use this layout, the pattern pieces cannot be wider than the width of the folded fabric.

To fold the fabric on the *crosswise grain,* align the raw edges together, folding the fabric in half to form a cross-grain fold. This layout accommodates wider pattern pieces, but not those requiring a fold.

The *gate fold* is a double fold, and is determined by the width of the pattern pieces. It is used when the pattern includes a number of pieces that require a fold position. Measure an equal distance from the selvage to determine the crosswise width and fold along the lengthwise grain.

When the pattern piece is too wide to be accommodated on the fold of the fabric, as in circular skirts, the lower corner is pieced along the lengthwise grain. Add seam allowance so that the pieces can be joined properly.

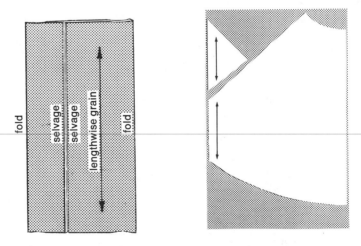

Gate Fold—Lengthwise Grain   Circular Skirts

Layout for Fabrics Requiring Special Handling

Napped fabrics, satins, plaids, stripes, one-way designs, large prints, and border patterns need extra yardage and require special layouts.

Napped or pile fabrics have a brushed or raised surface and the pattern pieces must be laid out in one direction. The surfaces of velvet, velveteen, corduroy, panne velvet, synthetic suede, fleece, camel's hair, and some flannels are smooth in one direction and rough in the opposite direction. Laying the pattern so that the rough texture runs downward gives a richer color to these fabrics. Lengthwise or gate folds are suitable for pattern layout on napped fabrics. If more width is necessary, cut the fabric on the cross grain, then layer the fabric, right sides together, with the nap following the same direction on both pieces.

Satin reflects the light and "shades off," appearing a different color when it is cut in different directions. Therefore, the pattern pieces must be cut in one direction.

Plaid fabrics are printed or woven and are designed evenly or unevenly. When pattern pieces are laid out on plaids or stripes they must be matched at the seam line and corresponding crossmarks. *Even plaids* are the same in both directions; this design creates a perfect alignment and is simple to match. To lay out a pattern on an even plaid, fold the fabric on either the lengthwise or the crosswise grain, matching the plaids of both layers. Pin through both layers at 4-inch intervals to prevent slipping.

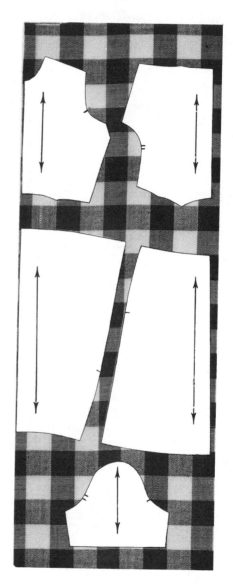

Even Plaid

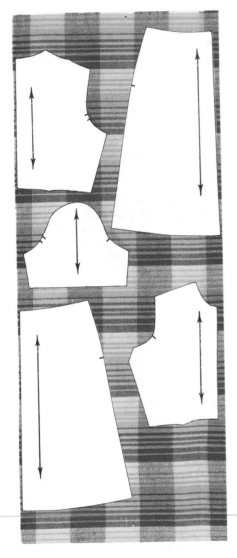

One-Way Plaid

A *one-way plaid* is uneven in the length-wise direction only. Pattern pieces are laid out in one direction. This type of plaid may be folded lengthwise or cut on the cross grain and realigned with the right sides together.

As *uneven plaid* is uneven both horizontally and vertically. It is simplest to lay out a pattern on a single thickness of an uneven plaid. The pattern of a garment to be laid out on this type of plaid should have a duplicate of each pattern piece needed to construct the garment. Position the pattern pieces on the right side of the fabric along the matching crosswise grain line, in order to keep the design balanced. This procedure will aid in mitering seams. It is extremely difficult to interlock pattern pieces and still match style lines and seams.

Striped fabrics are printed or woven, balanced or unbalanced, horizontal or vertical. Stripes are easy to match, as they run in only one direction. Follow the same layout preparation as for one-way or even plaids.

Large, bold, and widely spaced designs are placed so that they either balance on the body or give a pleasing effect to the eye. Garments with a minimum number of seams are best for large-scale designs, which must be matched at the style lines and seams.

Border patterns are woven or printed parallel to the selvage. In what is usually the most effective design, the pattern is placed on the crosswise grain with the border along the hem or sleeve edge. If the border is used vertically, it is best to avoid a waistline seam in order not to distort the border pattern at the hem.

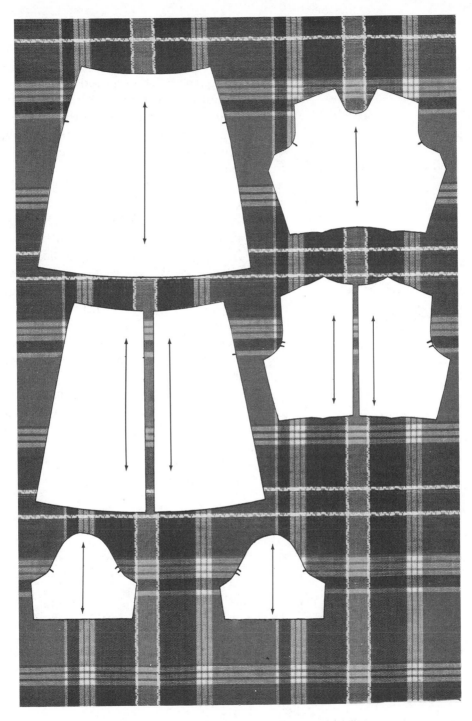

Uneven Plaid

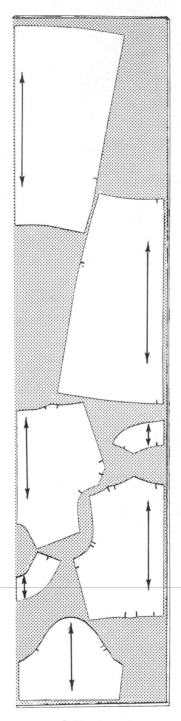

Cutting Layout

Pinning and Cutting

Select the fold suitable for the fabric and the garment styling, and make a trial layout before pinning by laying out the larger pattern pieces on the fabric, following the grainlines and pattern markings and interlocking the smaller pieces when possible.

When the best layout has been decided upon, pin the pattern pieces to the fabric (to prevent sheer, soft, and slippery fabrics from slipping, sandwich the fabric between layers of paper). Place the pins parallel to the seam line in the seam allowance area 5–6 inches apart on large pieces. Placing pins within the garment area can make holes and damage some delicate fabrics (satins, taffetas, velvets.) For the same reason, avoid pinning along the fold.

After the pattern layout is pinned, cut carefully along the outer edge of each piece. Clip in ⅛ inch at the crossmarks.

MARKING

Carboning

Carbon trace pattern pieces with the tracing wheel. Use white carbon paper for all fabrics, although light colored or white fabrics do not reflect the white carbon unless a great deal of pressure is applied on the tracing wheel. Colored graphite paper available in art supply stores is a good substitute for carbon paper: pressing lightly on the wheel will leave a pale impression of the graphite. Place each pattern piece on a carbon sheet and trace, following the seamlines. Remove the pattern; re-pin the two layers of fabric. In order to carbon the opposite layer, follow the carbon traced lines of the first marking.

Thread Tracing

Separate the pieces and thread trace. For thread tracing, use nylon, silk, or other continuous filament thread to prevent residue from remaining in the garment. The color of the thread should contrast slightly with that of the fabric.

Mark centers and construction details, and thread trace each seam to the raw edge, carefully intersecting all corners, so that a cross is visible on the right side of the fabric. Make crossmarks with a tiny running stitch.

Uneven basting, a combination of long and short stitches with the short stitch visible on the right side, is often used for thread tracing in curved areas.

PRESSING

To give a garment a professionally finished appearance, pressing as you sew is vital. Use of the proper equipment will make pressing simpler. To maintain the shape of the garment, press over the shaped pad, mitt, or roll. Set the iron at the desired heat and moisture, and cover the ironing board surface with muslin or canvas. All fabrics should be pressed on the wrong side; use a self-fabric press cloth on the right side when pressing on the wrong side is not feasible.

Test the iron on the wrong side of a sample piece of fabric.

Unless otherwise directed, remove all pins, thread tracings, and bastings before pressing.

After stitching each seam, press it closed to smooth the stitches. In order to press the seam allowance open and flat, first finger press by drawing your finger nail along the seamline.

To prevent the seam allowance from making ridge marks on the right side, use a piece of oaktag or tissue paper underneath the seam allowance as you press the seams open. When there are seams where top stitching is desired, press the seam allowance together and to the side where the decorative stitching is to be made.

Darts are pressed over a tailor's ham or the edge of the ironing board just to the tip of the vanishing point. Vertical darts are pressed toward the center of the garment, and horizontal darts are pressed down. With a heavy fabric, the dart pickup is cut open to within a safe distance from the vanishing point, and then trimmed and pressed open.

Princess line seams can be pressed together and toward the center.

To press gathers without flattening them, use the tip of the iron.

As the garment section is assembled, the shoulder and side seams are pressed open.

Collar, cuffs, and pocket details are given a firm pressing before being attached.

After armholes and waistline seams are stitched, the seam allowance is pressed together with the tip of the iron just touching the seamline.

Close zippers before pressing and use a press cloth.

Press hems lightly on the inside, avoiding a sharp crease at the hemline and a ridge at the sewing line.

After completion of the garment, give it a final pressing on the wrong side to eliminate any remaining wrinkles.

AN OVERVIEW OF SAMPLE ROOM PROCEDURES

In the sample room, each garment is a creation of its own and is handled on an individual basis. Commercial patterns are not used: the designer or the assistant drapes a pattern in muslin or develops an original pattern on paper. The assistant designer and sample hands drape, sew, and fit the garments created by the designer, and the designer or the assistant checks the fit of the samples as they are constructed.

After the pattern is developed and the muslin fitted on the dress form, it is cut in fabric. At the same time, all linings, underlinings, and interfacings are also prepared. All pieces are then carefully carbon traced, interfaced and thread traced, where necessary. The garment is then completely basted for its first fitting. Once this fitting is approved, any necessary alterations are made and the garment is refitted.

All necessary corrections are made and the stitching of the garment begins. All the basting necessary for the first fitting, which will interfere with correct sewing and pressing, is now removed. The essentials of correct garment construction should be observed during the assembling of each unit, including the use of correct basting and tracing stitches and proper pressing and handling.

While basting and stitching the garment sections, care should be taken to keep these units wrinkle-free. Overpressing to smooth out creases or wrinkles often spoils the garment's professional finish. As parts of the garment are assembled, place them on the dress form or on a hanger to help eliminate overhandling.

At least four fittings are required during the assembling. After darts, shoulders, side seams, and waistlines are joined and pressed, collars and facings are inserted, and sleeves are basted, a fitting is necessary. The next fitting will involve trimmings, pockets, and zipper. At this fitting, the length of the sleeves is checked and a hem is marked. When these steps are finished, and the garment is accessorized (belt, buttons, etc.), the final fitting takes place.

In some dress and sportswear concerns, the procedure varies with the garment being partially stitched before the first fitting. Necklines are staystitched to prevent stretching. All darts, side and shoulder seams are stitched. Waistlines are machine basted. Collars and sleeves are completed but not inserted for the first fitting. The fittings may be made on a dress form rather than on a model.

After the body of the garment is checked, the sleeves and collar are inserted and refitted and a hem is marked. The garment is then completed for the final try on.

3
Assembly

A SUMMARY OF ASSEMBLING PROCEDURES

For professional results, a systematic approach to the construction of a garment is essential. The procedures are presented here briefly, in the proper order for each type of garment.

Assembling Procedures for a Dress

1. Carbon and thread trace. Baste the underlining.

2. Baste the interfacing.

3. Baste the garment: seams, shirring, darts, etc.

4. First fitting—remove unnecessary basting.

5. Staystitch stress points and the neckline.

6. Make bound buttonholes.

7. Stitch and press the darts and seams. Insert in-seam pockets before the seams are joined.

8. Join the waist to the skirt.

9. Make the collar, cuffs, belt, and pockets.

10. Prepare the facings.

11. Apply the collar.

12. Attach the facings, sandwiching the collar.

13. Prepare the sleeves; finish the openings and apply the cuffs (if the length needs adjusting, the cuff is applied after the sleeve is mounted and fitted). Set the sleeves into the armholes and baste.

14. Second fitting.

15. Baste the pockets and trimming into place.

16. Stitch the zipper.

17. Stitch and finish the sleeves.

18. Third fitting—mark the hem.

19. Stitch the pockets.

20. Sew the hem.

21. Complete bound buttonholes; make machine or hand-worked buttonholes.

22. Final touches—buttons, hooks, eyes, belts, top or decorative stitching.

23. Final try on.

Assembling Procedures for a Blouse

1. Carbon and thread trace.

2. Baste the interfacing. If self-faced, interfacing is attached to the facing.

3. Baste the garment.

4. First fitting—remove unnecessary basting.

5. Staystitch stress points and the neckline.

6. Make bound buttonholes.

7. Stitch and press the darts and seams.

8. Make the collar, cuffs, and pockets.

9. Prepare the facing.

10. Apply the collar.

11. Attach the facing, sandwiching the collar.

12. Stitch the sleeves, finish the opening, and apply the cuffs.

13. Set and baste the sleeves into the armholes.

14. Baste the pockets, trimmings, and zipper.

15. Second fitting.

16. Stitch the pockets, sleeves into armholes, trimmings, and zipper.

17. Sew the bottom edge. If the garment is an overblouse, finish with a hem. For a blouse to be tucked in, stitch and pink the edge.

18. Complete bound buttonholes; make machine or hand-worked buttonholes.

19. Final touches—buttons, hooks, eyes, snaps, ties, top stitching.

20. Final try on.

Assembling Procedures for a Shirt

1. Carbon and thread trace.

2. Baste the interfacing to the front facings, shirtband, and collar.

3. Baste the garment and only one layer of the shoulder yoke.

4. First fitting—remove unnecessary basting.

5. Staystitch the neckline.

6. Join the yoke to the front and back of the shirt.

7. Stitch and press the side seams.

8. Make the collar, cuffs, pockets and sleeves.

9. Attach the front facing or suitable band or placket.

10. Attach the collar.

11. Set and baste the sleeves into the armholes.

12. Baste the pockets.

13. Second fitting.

14. Stitch the sleeves and pockets.

15. Stitch the bottom edge.

16. Make machine or hand-worked buttonholes.

17. Final touches—buttons and top stitching.

18. Final try on.

Assembling Procedures for a Skirt

1. Carbon and thread trace; baste the underlining.

2. Baste the interfacing or ribbon to the waistband.

3. Baste the side seams, pleats, yokes, etc.

4. First fitting—remove unnecessary basting.

5. Make bound buttonholes.

6. Stitch and press the darts, seams, and pleats; insert in-seam pockets before the seams are joined.

7. Make the pockets, belt tabs, ties, and slip lining.

8. Prepare the facings.

9. Attach the facings.

10. Stitch the zipper.

11. Join the slip lining to the waistline.

12. Baste the pockets and waistband.

13. Second fitting—mark the hem.

14. Stitch the pockets and waistband.

15. Sew the hem.

16. Complete bound buttonholes; make machine or hand-worked buttonholes.

17. Final touches—top stitching, buttons, hooks, eyes, snaps, belts, ties.

18. Final try on.

Assembling Procedures for Slacks

1. Carbon and thread trace.

2. Baste the interfacing or ribbon to the waistband.

3. Baste the crotch seams, and trim the seams to ½ inch in the curved area.

4. Baste the side and inner leg seams.

5. First fitting—remove unnecessary basting.

6. Stitch and press the darts and seams. Insert in-seam pockets before seams are joined. Double stitch or tape the curved crotch seam.

7. Stitch the zipper.

8. Make the pockets, belt, tabs, and slip lining.

9. Join the slip lining to the waistline.

10. Baste the waistband and pockets.

11. Second fitting—mark the hem.

12. Stitch the waistband, tabs, and pockets.

13. Sew the hem.

14. Final touches—top stitching, hooks, eyes, buttons, buttonholes.

15. Final try on.

UNDERLINING

Underlining and fabric are cut exactly alike. Place each garment section and its underlining wrong sides together. Pin the two layers together, keeping them smooth and without puckers. Thread trace through the centers, darts, seam lines, buttonhole markings, and cross-marks. This thread tracing acts as a basting, and the joined fabrics are now treated as one during construction.

INTERFACING

Interfacings are applied to the garment before the seams are joined in order to minimize bulk.

1. When using woven or nonwoven interfacing, trim away all but a ¼ inch seam allowance beyond the seam line.

2. With woven or nonwoven press-on interfacing, trim away all but a ⅛ inch seam allowance beyond the seam line before applying to each garment section. Staystitching is not necessary but is recommended to reinforce stress point corners and angles.

3. When using fusible interfacings, trim away all but a ⅛ inch seam allowance beyond the seam line before applying to each garment section.

4. The fusible web and its accompanying fabric are cut to leave a ⅛ inch seam allowance beyond the seam line before applying to each garment section.

LINING

The lining is constructed as a separate unit. Slip linings are used in dresses, skirts, and slacks, where facings have been omitted. Dress sleeves are generally not lined. The lining hems in dresses, skirts, and slacks are finished separately from the exterior hems. To join a slip lining, attach the lining and garment, wrong sides together, at the neckline and armhole in dresses and at the waistline in skirts and slacks. At the zipper opening, turn the lining seam allowance to the wrong side and hem it to the zipper tape. Then attach the collar and sleeves in dresses and the waistband in skirts and slacks. Mark and complete the garment hem. Hem the lining 1 inch shorter than the garment, finishing it by hand or machine.

Where there are facings, as in jackets, vests, and dresses, the lining is hand finished to the facing. The sleeves are attached after the body lining is sewn into the garment. (Wearing ease has been allowed in the sleeve lining and at the hem of the lining.) To join the lining, attach lining and garment, wrong sides together, and turn under the seam allowance, matching the centers and seamlines. Turn up the hem shorter than the bottom of the garment. Pin, baste, and slip stitch the lining to the garment. The sleeve lining is attached to the garment around the armhole, matching crossmarks, and slip stitched into place. The bottom of the sleeve lining is turned under ½ inch shorter than the garment sleeve, and is slip stitched.

DARTS

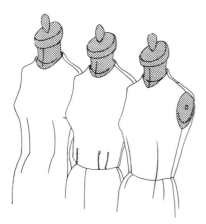

Darts are used to fit the garment to the contours of the body. To appear inconspicuous, they require a specific type of stitching, finishing, and pressing.

Darts may lie at any angle to the body. The basic darts are triangular, curved, double-pointed and the dart tuck.

Before stitching, a dart should always be pinned and basted, then fitted to the dress form or model. The stitching of a dart varies slightly, depending upon its shape. Accurate stitching, tapering to the vanishing point, insures an almost invisible blending of the stitching with the fabric. Begin by tacking and stitching waistline darts ⅜ inch beyond the intersecting seam, and stitch to the vanishing point, stitching the last few stitches on the folded edge. After stitching to the vanishing point, leave enough thread to tie a tailor's knot (tacking or back stitching thickens the point of a dart, so that the fabric will crush when pressed). Stitch underarm, shoulder, and neckline darts from the outer edge of the fabric to the vanishing point. A double-pointed dart must be tapered and knotted at both points. The dart tuck may be finished by stitching across the end to the fold or by tacking at the end of the seam.

Dart Type	Uses of Dart	Stitching	Trimming and Pressing	
triangular	front waist back waist shoulder sleeve neckline		horizontal	vertical
curved	front waist bust skirt front skirt back pants front pants back		slash and trim	open
double pointed	dress blouse		clip	
dart　　tuck	waist skirt blouse			

Darts do not need a seam finish unless the style of the dart or the thickness of the fabric necessitates trimming or splitting. For deep darts, trim away the excess fabric, leaving a ½ inch seam allowance. Darts in medium or heavy fabrics often require splitting to within ½ inch of the vanishing point before pressing open. In sheer fabrics a dart is finished as narrowly as a French seam: after stitching the dart, stitch a second row ⅛ inch away and trim the excess fabric close to the stitches. A double-pointed dart may need clipping so that it will lie smooth when pressed.

Always press darts flat before proceeding to turn them in the correct direction. All vertical darts or tucks are pressed toward the center of the body and horizontal or diagonal darts are pressed downward. Split and trimmed darts are pressed open. Care should be taken not to press beyond the vanishing point of the dart, thereby creasing the garment. Press all darts over a ham, mitt, or seam roll to maintain the shape of the garment. To prevent ridge marks on the right side, underpress the fold of the dart.

TUCKS

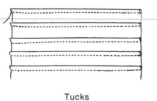

Tucks

Tucks are parallel folds of fabric used for a decorative effect on the right side of the fabric. The spacing can vary from the very narrow pin tucks to deeper, spaced tucks.

For perfection in stitching tucks, the markings must be exact. The pin tuck is an edge stitch evenly spaced $\frac{1}{16}$ inch from the fold; for wider or more widely spaced tucks, increase the amount of fabric in each fold or the space between the tucks. Where large amounts of tucking are needed, the fabric is sent to a commercial source. The garment pattern section is then positioned over the tucks and cut.

EASING, GATHERING, AND SHIRRING

Easing, gathering, and shirring are three methods of controlling fullness to various degrees and for different styles. The ease stitch is necessary when a slightly larger area or shaped edge must be joined to a smaller edge: the ease stitch avoids puckering. The use of gathering stitches in one or two rows draws up the fabric into fine pleat-like folds. Shirring is three or more rows of evenly spaced stitches that add a decorative touch to the garment while drawing in fullness.

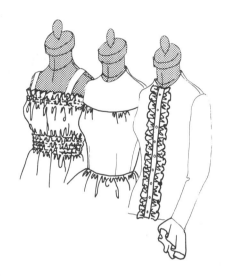

Easing

Sleeve caps, curved seams, and contour hems need a row of ease stitching to mold the shape of the garment. The most effective ease stitch is achieved by winding the machine bobbin with heavy-duty thread (size 40) and setting the machine at 8–10 stitches to the inch, depending upon the weight of the fabric. (the lighter the fabric, the smaller the stitch size). After stitching, draw up the bobbin thread to control the ease and distribute the fabric evenly.

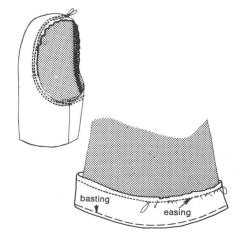

basting

easing

Gathering

Gathering a large amount of fullness into a small area requires two rows of machine stitching in the seam allowance area. The resulting stitching should not be visible on the right side when the two pieces of a garment are joined. The sewing machine should be set at 6–8 stitches to the inch, the stitch size depending upon the weight of the fabric and the amount of gathering necessary. The lighter the weight of the fabric, the smaller the stitch size. Again, it is advisable to wind the bobbin with heavy-duty thread (size 40), to prevent the gathering thread from breaking. With the right side of the garment facing up, stitch the first row of gathering next to the seam line and the second row ¼ inch into the seam allowance area.

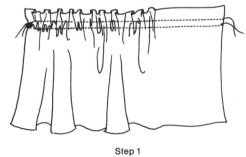

Step 1

Step 2

1. For ease of handling, divide the area to be gathered into sections and gather each section separately. Then draw up the bobbin threads and distribute the fullness evenly. To anchor the gathering threads, draw the top thread to the inside and tie with a tailor's knot.

2. Join garment pieces right sides together with the gathered area on top, placing pins perpendicular to the raw edges, matching the seam lines, and even baste with a small stitch between the two rows of gathering.

3. Machine stitch next to the gathering stitch, taking care to keep the non-gathered area smooth and the gathering stitch from showing and forming folds or pleats.

GATHERING FOOT ATTACHMENT. Make a sample before actually gathering: the gathering foot permanently locks the gathers and therefore you must pre-determine the stitch size and the amount of fullness desired. Change the machine to the largest stitch to gather the most fabric; the smaller stitch to gather less. The gathering foot, which does only one row of stitching, is most effective for ruffles or flounces.

RUFFLES. Ruffles add a soft, feminine effect to the neckline, sleeves, or hem of a garment. The grain, fullness, and finish of the ruffle will depend upon the weight of the fabric. Straight ruffles cut on grain or bias can be gathered to various degrees of fullness. To distribute the fullness evenly, use two rows of gathering with heavy-duty thread on the bobbin. After joining the ruffle to the garment, the joined edges may be cleanly finished with the addition of a facing or a bias strip, or with two rows of machine stitching and trimming away of the excess fabric.

single width ruffle

Straight ruffles cut *on grain* are cut singly with seam and hem allowances. A bias-cut ruffle may be cut singly or double. The double width in lightweight fabric has the advantage of a folded edge for the finish.

double width ruffle

Circular ruffles add fullness with or without gathers. The spiral ruffle, which has less flare, calls for the addition of gathers. The outer edges are machine or hand hemmed.

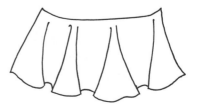

circular ruffle

Shirring

A decorative effect can be achieved with several rows of shirring; the use of a contrasting thread on the right side of the garment is effective. In areas where the shirring must be controlled, a stay is achieved by the use of a piece of fabric or twill tape attached by hand to the wrong side of the shirred area.

Shirring

Shirring With Stay

ELASTIC THREAD. For a flexible, close fit, use elastic thread in shirring. Wind the bobbin with elastic thread and easy tension, and then thread the bobbin case with reduced tension. This method precludes the necessity of drawing up the bobbin thread. Stitch multiple rows on the right side of the fabric until the desired width of shirring is achieved. Knot all threads on the inside to prevent unraveling. Some adjustment of the elastic thread may be needed, but care should be taken not to reduce elasticity.

PLEATS

The different types of pleats are made by folding the fabric in various ways. Side pleats are all turned in the same direction. Box pleats have the two folds turned away from each other. Inverted pleats, which have a separate underlay piece, have the two folds meeting at the center. All these pleats, when pressed, will give a trim, straight silhouette, and when unpressed, a soft, full silhouette. Accordian and sunburst pleats do not have any depth. Accordian pleats are cut on the straight and sunburst pleats are cut circularly. All-around, side, box, accordian, and sunburst pleats are made commercially, with the seams joined to allow sufficient width, and with the hems completed. The commercial pleater forms the pleats and shapes the waist and hip to the desired measurements. The skirt is completed by closing the seam, inserting the zipper, and applying the waistband.

If the pleats are not made commercially, they must be prepared with precision. They are completed before the seams, zipper, waistband, and hem are finished.

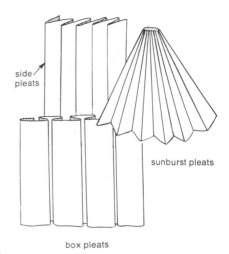

side pleats

sunburst pleats

box pleats

Box, Inverted and Side Pleats

1. For inverted and side pleats, machine baste the pleats, right sides together, from the waist to the hem.

2. For box pleats, machine baste the pleats, wrong sides together, from the waist to the hem.

3. For pleats that are partially stitched closed, set the machine at 12 stitches per inch and stitch from the waist to the point

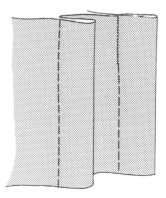

Steps 1-3

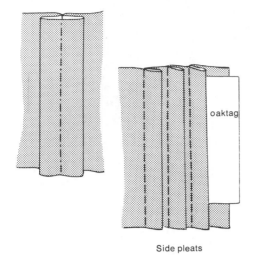

Side pleats

where the pleats open. Tack. Change to machine basting and continue stitching to the hem.

4. To press inverted or box pleats, refold each pleat evenly on each side of the stitching. For side pleats, press each pleat to one side of the stitching. Use a press cloth and oaktag to prevent ridges. Do not remove the basting until the pressing is completed.

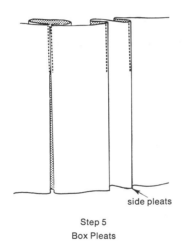

side pleats

Step 5
Box Pleats

5. For a decorative effect, edge or top stitch the part of a pleat that is stitched closed. Draw the top thread through to the wrong side and tie.

Inverted Pleats with a Separate Underlay

1. For the inverted pleat that is open to the waist, machine baste the pleat, right sides together, from the waist to the hem.

2. For the pleat that is partially closed and has a shaped underlay, stitch the seam 2 inches below the point where the underlay will be positioned. Then machine baste the rest of the way to the hem.

3. Press the pleat open.

4. Position the pleat and the underlay piece, right sides together. Baste and stitch the pleat and underlay together. Remove the basting.

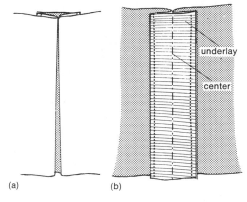

(a)   (b)

Inverted Pleat With Underlay

5. To hold a shaped underlay with a partially closed pleat, top stitch the pleat on the right side. Remove the basting.

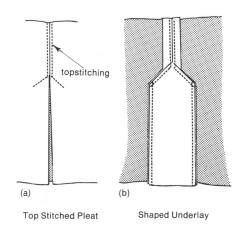

topstitching

(a)   (b)

Top Stitched Pleat   Shaped Underlay

YOKES

Yokes are small parts of a garment that create a styled line when joined to the body of the garment. Yokes are used at the neckline, shoulder, or hip line. They are cut double and are cleanly finished on the inside of the yoke lining. The use of backing is optional.

Neckline Yoke

1. Join shoulder seams of the yoke and yoke lining.

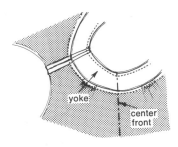

Steps 1-3

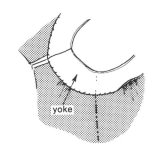

Step 4

2. Join the yoke to the front and back of the garment along the yoke style line.

3. Join the yoke lining to the garment at the neckline, right sides together (if a collar is desired, sandwich it between the yoke and the yoke lining). Baste stitch, trim the seam in layers, and clip around the neckline. Turn the yoke lining to the inside of the garment.

4. To complete the yoke lining, turn under the raw edge and hand stitch or crack stitch along the yoke style line.

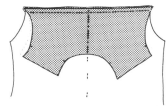

Step 1

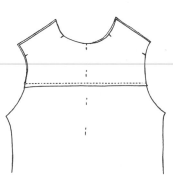

Steps 2 & 3

Shirt Yoke

In constructing a shirt yoke, unlike the neckline yoke, the back yoke style line is cleanly finished in one step.

1. Place the yoke and garment right sides together. Place the right side of the yoke lining against the wrong side of the garment.

2. Baste, stitch, and trim.

3. Press the yokes together to enclose the seam of the shirt.

4. If desired, top stitch or edge stitch along the back yoke seam line.

There are three methods for attaching the front yoke.

METHOD 1

1. Baste the right side of the yoke lining to the wrong side of the shirt front. Roll up the front and the back of the shirt and sandwich them between the front yokes, right sides together. Baste, stitch, and trim.

2. Turn the shirt to the right side through the neckline.

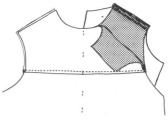

Method 1

METHOD 2

1. To finish the front yoke on the right side, pin the right side of the yoke lining to the wrong side of the garment. Baste, stitch, and trim.

2. Fold under the raw edge of the yoke seam allowance and pin and baste, covering the machine stitching, and edge stitch.

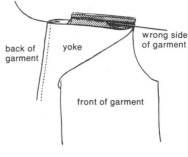

Method 2

METHOD 3

1. To finish the front yoke on the wrong side by hand or crack stitching, pin the yoke and garment right sides together. Baste, stitch, and trim.

2. Fold under the raw edge of the yoke lining and hand hem or crack stitch.

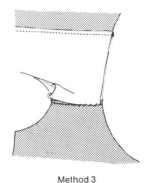

Method 3

Hipline Yokes

A skirt or slack yoke is always lined.

1. Baste and stitch the yoke seams and the garment seams, leaving an opening for the zipper.

2. With the right sides together, baste and stitch the yoke to the skirt or slacks.

3. Insert the zipper.

4. Stitch the seams of the yoke lining.

5. For a garment with a waistband, attach the yoke lining to the garment, wrong sides together, and baste along the waistline.

For a garment without a waistband, interface the waistline area of the yoke and join the lining to the waistline, right sides together. Stitch, trim, clip, and turn the lining to the inside of the garment.

6. Turn under the raw edge of the lining ½ inch and hem along the yoke style line; hem the edges of the lining to the zipper tape.

7. Attach the waistband.

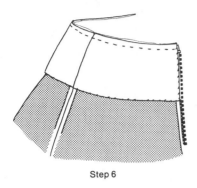

Step 6

JOINING WAIST AND SKIRT

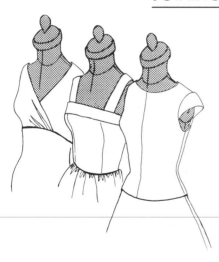

When joining a waist and skirt, the joined seam can be at the natural waistline, the empire line, or a dropped waistline. The joining is completed after the waist and skirt have been stitched and before the collar, sleeves, and zipper are inserted.

Note that the stitching of darts and seams extends ⅜ inch beyond the waistline intersection.

If the skirt is slightly larger than the waist, a row of ease stitching is necessary along the waistline thread tracing. Draw up the ease to allow for fitting the waist to the skirt.

1. Join the waist and the skirt, right sides together, along the waistline thread tracing, matching the seams, centers, and crossmarks. Pin, baste, and stitch along the waistline thread tracing, with any gathers on top.

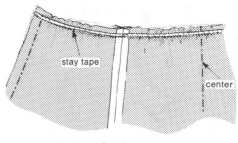

Step 3

2. Remove all thread tracings and bastings.

3. To prevent stretching and relieve stress on the waistline, either stitch a stay tape into the seam allowance along the waistline seam, or add a second row of stitching along the joined waistline seam.

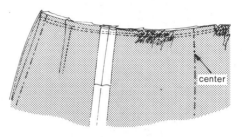

Step 3

4. Trim the seam allowance, leaving the waist edge wider than the skirt edge.

5. Press the seam allowance flat, just touching the seam line, and turn the seam upward into the waist.

POCKETS

Pockets are garment details that add design interest or act as a functional part of the garment. Pockets may be inserted into the garment and finished like buttonholes, with welts or flaps. They may be hidden in seams or applied to the outside of the garment.

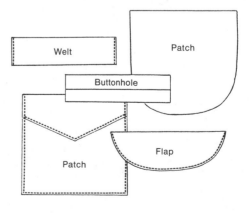

Patch Pocket—Lined or Unlined

A patch pocket may be round or square and may be attached to the garment by machine or hand stitching.

UNLINED PATCH POCKET

1. Finish the top edge of the pocket with an edge stitch or with stitching and pinking.

2. Fold over the hem, right sides together, and stitch ends closed. Clip and turn the hem.

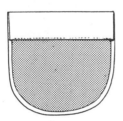

Steps 1 & 2

3. When the pocket is rounded at the lower edge, turn the seam allowance to the wrong side and press.

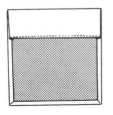

Step 3

4. When the pocket is square, clip the corners and turn the seam allowance to the wrong side and press.

5. See below, Attaching Patch Pockets.

Step 4

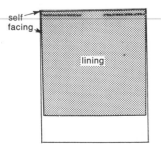

self facing

lining

LINED POCKET WITH A SELF FACING

1. Cut the lining slightly smaller than the pocket.

2. Baste the lining to the self facing, right sides together. Stitch, leaving a 1 inch opening on this seam for turning.

Steps 1 & 2

3. Fold the pocket and lining, right sides together, and stitch along the seamline.

4. Trim the seam allowance, clipping corners and notching curves. Notch the curved pocket fabric and the lining alternately to insure a smooth edge.

Step 3

5. Turn the pocket to the right side through the 1 inch opening and hand stitch the lining to the pocket facing.

6. Roll the seam line slightly to the wrong side and uneven baste. Remove the basting before pressing and attaching the pocket to the garment.

7. See below, Attaching Patch Pockets.

Step 5

LINED POCKET

1. Cut the lining slightly smaller than the pocket.

2. Baste the pocket and lining, right sides together, matching the raw edges.

3. Stitch around the entire pocket.

4. Trim the seam allowance, clipping corners and notching curves alternately to insure a smooth edge.

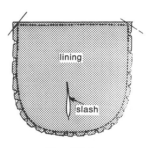

Steps 3 & 4

5. In order to turn the pocket to the right side, slash through the lining for 1 inch near the lower edge of the pocket.

6. Turn the pocket to the right side, and close the slash with a catch stitch.

7. Roll the seamline slightly to the wrong side and uneven baste. Remove the basting before pressing and attaching the pocket to the garment.

8. See below, Attaching Patch Pockets.

Step 5

71

Edge Stitching

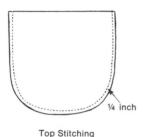

¼ inch

Top Stitching

ATTACHING PATCH POCKETS. The method used to attach patch pockets to the garment depends upon the finish desired. For sportswear or casual wear, machine stitching is usually used. Where top stitching is undesirable, the pockets are attached with hand stitching.

Edge stitching or top stitching are two methods of machine stitching pockets to garments. The top edge of a pocket must be securely attached and the threads drawn through to the wrong side and knotted. Place the pocket in position on the garment. Pin and baste. Then edge stitch, starting at the upper edge and reinforcing the pocket with a triangle for a decorative effect; or top stitch ¼ inch away from the edge to form a lip around the edge of the pocket. When the pocket is made out of heavy fabric, complete the top stitching before attaching the pocket to the garment, and then attach the pocket by hand.

To attach the pocket by hand and insure invisible stitching, baste the pocket into position ¼ inch from the outer edge. Then back stitch on the inside of the garment, using the basting as a guide and picking up only the lining or the seam allowance of the pocket close to the basting.

Slip stitching can also be used to attach pockets. On the right side of the garment, turn back the edge of the pocket. Slip stitch slightly inside the edge of the pocket, picking up the lining or the seam allowance of the pocket

Welt and Flap Pockets

Welt and flap pockets are constructed similarly, with the difference in appearance that the welt stands upward and the flap hangs downward. The flap pocket has a narrow welt concealed beneath the flap.

1. Reinforce the pocket position on the garment by basting a piece of interfacing 3 inches wide and 2 inches longer than the opening on the wrong side.

2. Interface the welt or flap. For a one-piece welt or flap, cut the interfacing ½ inch past the horizontal center line, and catch stitch it to the wrong side of the fabric.

3. Fold the welt or flap right sides together and stitch. Trim the ends, turn, and press. Baste the raw edges together with ¼ inch seam allowance. The flap pocket has a narrow welt: prepare a strip of fabric ¾ inch wide and the length of the pocket, plus seam allowance.

4. The two-piece flap may be faced with a lightweight or lining fabric. The facing is slightly smaller than the upper flap. Stitch, clip, and turn to the right side.

5. Press the flap, rolling the seam to the underside, and baste the raw edges together with a ¼ inch seam allowance.

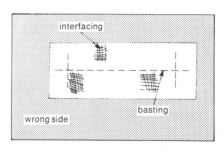

Step 2

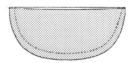

Step 3

Steps 4 & 5
Welt and Flap Pockets

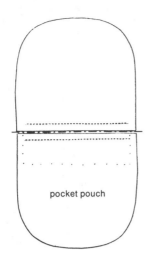

pocket pouch

For the welt pocket: on the right side of the garment, pin the welt into position with the raw edges facing up. Place the smaller pocket pouch section right side down over the welt. Place the larger pouch section right side down, meeting the raw edge of the welt. Baste and stitch the width of the welt, using a ¼ inch seam allowance and tack securely.

welt

For the flap pocket: on the right side of the garment, pin the flap into position, right side down, with the raw edges facing down. Pin the narrow welt facing up meeting the raw edge of the flap. Place the larger pouch section right side down over the flap, and the smaller pouch section over the welt. Baste and stitch the width of the flap and welt with a ¼ inch seam allowance, tacking securely.

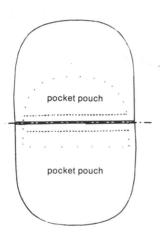

pocket pouch

pocket pouch

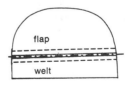

flap

welt

Step 7

7. To complete the welt or flap pocket, cut the pocket opening on the garment to within ½ inch of each end, and then clip diagonally into each corner, forming a triangle on each end.

8. Pull the pocket pieces to the wrong side.

9. Turn the welt up and the flap down. The narrow welt on the flap pocket will face up. Press the upper seams open and press the welt and flap into position.

10. Match the pouch edges. With the triangles lying flat, stitch around the pouch sections, catching the triangles and tacking securely. The narrow welt on the flap pocket is stitched to the pouch at this time.

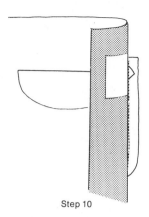

Step 10

11. Finish the welt invisibly by hand with a back stitch on the inside, or edge stitch on the right side.

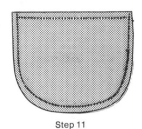

Step 11

Double Welt or Buttonhole Pockets

Double welt or buttonhole pockets are constructed in the same way as bound buttonholes. The difference is in the length of the welts or buttonhole strips. Prepare the welts with a ¼ inch seam allowance. In the center of the pocket, mark three lines. Space the outer two lines so that the distance between them is twice the desired finished width of the welt.

1. Welts may be cut on lengthwise or bias grain. For each welt cut two strips the length of the pocket width plus 1 inch.

Double Welt or Buttonhole Pocket

2. Thread trace the pocket width on each strip.

3. Pin the welts, aligning the thread tracing with the edge of the pocket marking on the garment. Baste on the welt seam line.

Pocket Marking

4. Stitch the length of each welt, tacking at both ends. Check the wrong side to be sure the stitches are parallel.

5. Remove all thread tracings and bastings.

6. Cut through the center of the garment and interfacing to within ⅜ inch of each end, and clip diagonally into each corner.

7. Pull the welts to the wrong side and position the edges to meet at the center. Baste together closely.

8. Fold the garment back, exposing on each side the triangle left by the clipping. Center the strips, stitch, and tack the triangles to the welt.

9. Press lightly on the wrong side.

10. Place the large pouch section against the upper welt, and the smaller pouch section against the lower welt. Stitch to the seam allowance, using a cording foot.

11. To finish, follow steps 10 and 11 of the directions for finishing the pouch of the welt and flap pockets.

Front Hip Pockets

Front hip pockets are part of the cutaway areas of skirts and pants. Complete the pocket before joining the seams of the garment or attaching the waistband.

1. Interface the upper curved edge of the pocket on the garment.

2. Pin, baste, and stitch the pocket facing to the garment, right sides together.

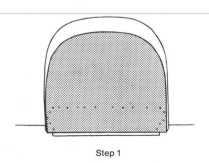

Step 1

3. Trim the seam allowance in layers, and clip the curve.

4. Turn the facing to the wrong side and roll the seam to the inside of the facing. Press. If desired, top stitch along the edge or back stitch the facing.

5. Pin the back pocket section to the facing, right sides together, matching the outer edges. Stitch around the curved outer edge of the pocket section.

6. To hold the pocket in place, baste along the waistline and side seams.

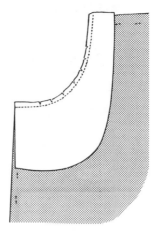

Steps 2 & 3

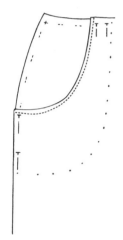

Steps 4 & 5

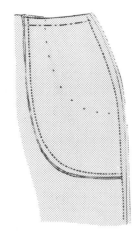

Steps 5 & 6

Inseam Pockets

The inseam pocket is hidden in the side or princess seam of a garment; it is suitable for skirts, slacks, and dresses. The pouch can be made of self-fabric or lining. When using lining, apply a 2 inch strip of self-fabric to the back seam allowance. In order to prevent stretching on bias seams, staystitch a piece of tape along the seam

77

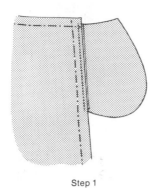

Step 1

line in the seam allowance area. The pocket shape varies slightly for dresses.

1. Pin, baste, and stitch the front and back pocket pouch to the seams of the garment with ¼ inch seam allowance. The joined seams should not be visible from the outside of the garment. Press the seam allowance toward the pocket pouch.

Steps 2 & 3

2. When inserting the pocket into the seam, stitch the garment along the seam line to 1 inch below the top of the pocket.

3. Pin the pouch pieces together, matching the raw edges. Stitch the outer edge of the pouch to the seam intersection, and continue stitching along the seam line of the garment to the hem edge.

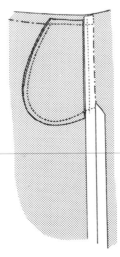

Step 4

4. Turn the pouch toward the center front of the garment. Clip into the back seam allowance of the garment, and press the seam open.

5. For skirts or slacks, baste the top edge of the pocket to the waistline to hold it in place before attaching the waistband

BIAS

Bias is a flexible, decorative, and functional finish or trim for necklines, collars, cuffs, armholes, style lines, pockets and raw edges. It varies in width and is often used in a contrasting color and fabric. Bias can be made into binding, facing, piping, spaghetti, and loops.

Cutting Bias

Take the lengthwise grain and fold it parallel to the crosswise grain. The folded edge connecting the opposite corners is the true bias. Draw a diagonal line connecting the corners. Mark lines parallel to the diagonal line as wide as the bias strips are to be cut, including seam allowances. Mark the lengthwise grain for joining the strips.

When using bias strips for binding, use a single thickness for heavy fabrics and a double thickness for light or medium fabrics. Single bias is cut twice the desired finished width, plus seam allowance. Double bias is cut four times the desired finished width, plus seam allowance, and then folded in half, right sides out. Bias used as binding is usually finished no wider than ¾ inch. To estimate the width of bias needed to encase cording, measure a piece of fabric folded over the cord and add ¼ inch seam allowance on each edge.

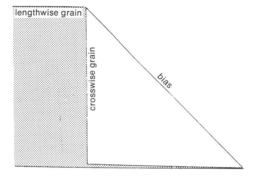

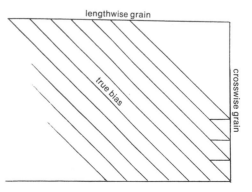

Finished Bias Strip	Width to Cut	
	Single	Double
¼	1	1½
⅜	1¼	2
½	1½	2½
⅝	1¾	3
¾	2	3½

Joining Bias Strips

1. Bias strips that have been separately must be joined on the lengthwise grain. Join the strips, right sides together, at right angles to each other with a ¼ inch seam allowance. The strips will overlap at the corners but the seam lines will match. Press the seams open and clip away the points that extend.

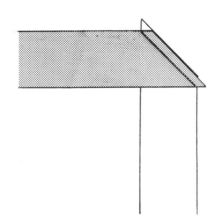

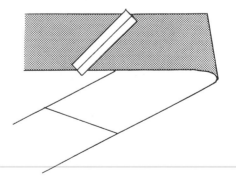

2. For a continuous bias strip that has been joined before cutting, mark the true bias line and width lines on the wrong side of a precut block of bias fabric. Pin right sides together, extending one edge of the fabric the width of one strip. Stitch the lengthwise seam. Press the seam allowance open and cut a continuous strip.

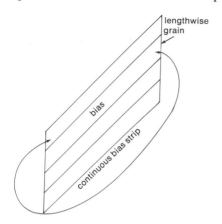

lengthwise grain

bias

continuous bias strip

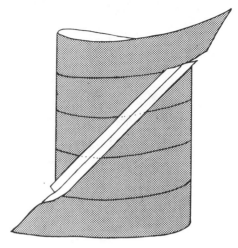

Single and Double Bias Binding

1. For single bias, pin the raw edge of the binding to the garment, right sides together, and stitch.

2. Turn the binding to the wrong side, encasing the seam allowance.

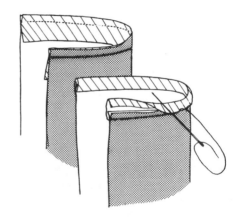

Steps 2 & 3

3. Turn under the raw edge ¼ inch and hand hem, picking up the machine stitches, or crack stitch by machine, using the binding foot.

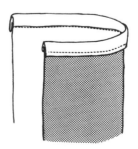

Step 3

Step 4

4. For double bias, fold the strip, wrong sides together, and join the raw edges of the garment and the binding, right sides together. The folded edge eliminates having to turn under the raw edge for hemming.

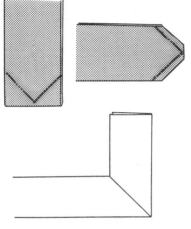

Corners, Inward Miter

CURVES AND CORNERS. For perfect application of bias binding, curves and corners must be specially handled.

When applying single or double bindings to curves, the bias must be stretched slightly on inside curves (as in necklines), and eased on outside curves (as in collars).

To apply binding with inside and outside corners, it is necessary to predetermine the length of the binding and the exact point where the corners meet. Cut single bias strips for ease in handling.

1. Fold the bias on the width, right sides together, and form the two ends into a right angle. Stitch, trim, press, and turn to the right side.

2. Pin one layer of the binding to the right side of the garment and stitch, using a ¼ inch seam allowance.

3. Turn under the raw edge of the binding to encase the seam allowance and hand hem, picking up the machine stitches, or crack stitch by machine.

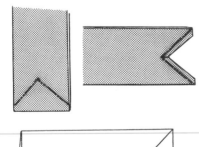

Corners, Outward Miter

Bias Facing

Bias facing is used to finish the raw edges of necklines and armholes on either the right or the wrong side of the garment.

1. Using single bias 1 inch wide, pin the bias to the garment, matching the raw edges.

2. Stitch, with a ¼ inch seam allowance, and clip.

3. Turn the bias strip and roll the seam edge under.

4. To finish, turn under the raw edge ¼ inch and edge stitch.

5. Top stitch the outer edge.

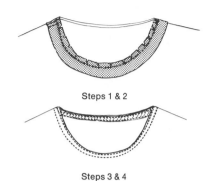

Steps 1 & 2

Steps 3 & 4

Piping

1. To prepare piping with or without cord, cut strips of bias the length needed and wide enough to cover the cord, plus seam allowance.

2. Fold each strip in half, wrong sides together, encasing the cord.

3. Machine stitch with a cording foot, stretching the bias slightly. Do not catch the cord when stitching.

4. For uncorded piping, pull out the cord.

5. To insert the piping between two layers of fabric, place the piping on the right side of the garment, matching the raw edges.

6. Align the stitching of the piping along the seam line of the garment and baste.

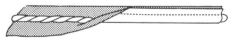

Steps 1 & 2

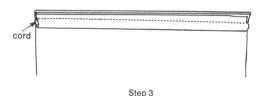

cord

Step 3

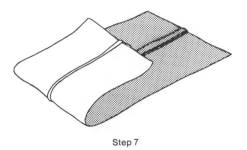

Step 7

7. Join the garment section and facing right sides together, sandwiching the piping, and stitch along the seam line of the garment.

8. For easier handling of curves and corners, clip into the seam allowance of the piping as necessary while stitching.

Noncorded Spaghetti Tubing

1. To prepare spaghetti without cord, cut the bias strip the desired length.

2. The width of the bias, including the seam allowance, depends on the type of fabric, because the seam allowance becomes the filler for the spaghetti.

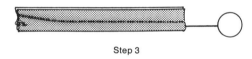

Step 3

3. To facilitate easy turning, stitch with small stitches, right sides together, slightly stretching the bias. Begin stitching at the raw edge, angling toward the seam line, and continue stitching. Do not trim the seam allowance.

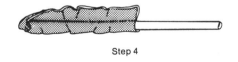

Step 4

4. To reverse the fabric, slide a loop turner through the tube and lock the end. Draw the fabric through to turn to the right side.

Corded Spaghetti Tubing

1. To prepare corded spaghetti, cut the bias strip the desired length and wide enough to encase the cord, plus a seam allowance.

2. Cut the cord twice the length of the bias strip.

3. Encase the cord in the bias strip (right sides together) and secure the bias strip at the center of the cord by stitching securely.

4. To facilitate easy turning of the cord, use a cording foot and small stitches, slightly stretching the bias. Begin stitching at the raw edge, angling toward the cord, and continue to stitch along the entire length of the cord. Do not catch the cord.

5. Trim the seam allowance to ⅛ inch. To turn, gently draw the fabric over the exposed cord until the entire strip of fabric covers the cord.

6. Cut off the excess cord.

Loops

A suitable closing for buttons are loops made out of narrow tubing or spaghetti. The amount of spaghetti needed depends on the size of the button, plus a seam allowance. The loops are attached to the right front center of the garment, and the left front is cut with an extension. Single loops are cut separately and spaced evenly apart from one another; continuous loops hug one another.

1. A paper guide is necessary for accurate marking. Mark two lengthwise grain lines, one for the center and the other for the depth of the loop.

2. Mark the width of the loops.

3. Form loops from the spaghetti, with the seam line on the inside of the curve, and machine baste the loops close to the center guide line on the paper.

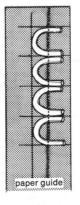

Steps 1-3

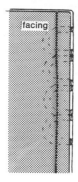

Steps 4-6

4. Baste the paper guide over the right center front on the right side of the garment. Stitch on the center guide line.

5. Tear the paper away. Pin and baste the facing to the garment, right sides together, sandwiching the loops.

6. Stitch on the center line.

Step 7

7. Trim the loops and the seam allowance. Turn and press (do not press the loops, but press the facing on the wrong side). The loops will extend from the edge of the garment.

8. Place the buttons on the center line of the left half of the garment.

Inserted Bias Trim

An inserted bias finish is suitable when the bias trim is seen only on the right side of the garment and no visible machine stitch on the bias is desired. The inserted bias trim is found at the edges of collars, cuffs, and patch pockets and along the outer edges of garments.

When the desired bias trim finish is ½ inch, cut single bias strips 1 inch wide. The upper collar, cuff, pocket, or garment is cut away ½ inch at the outer edge to reduce bulk. When the upper collar, cuff, pocket, or garment is interfaced, the interfacing will extend ½ inch beyond the edge.

1. Pin, baste, and stitch the bias to the edge of the garment, right sides together. Follow the instructions for curves and corners, using a ¼ inch seam allowance.

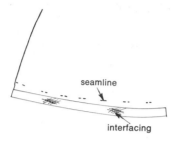

seamline

interfacing

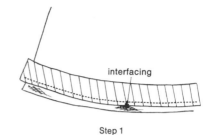

interfacing

Step 1

2. Turn the bias to cover the seam allowances and align the raw edges of the interfacing and the bias. Baste and press.

3. Complete the finish of the raw edge with the under collar, facing, or pocket lining.

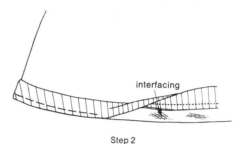

interfacing

Step 2

FACINGS

Facings finish the raw edges of necklines, armholes, sleeves, and contour edges. The facing is cut on the lengthwise, crosswise, or bias grain, depending upon the edge faced. Lightweight fabrics are used to face heavyweight fabrics. A facing may be shaped, combination, or self, and areas requiring facings should be interfaced. Interfacings are selected in relation to the shape of the garment, the firmness desired, and the weight of the fabric.

If a zipper is part of the garment construction, a lapped or centered zipper is inserted after the facing is completed;

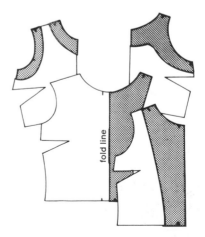

fold line

an invisible zipper is stitched to the garment before the facing is attached.

Neckline Facing

Complete the facing before joining it to the garment:

1. Stitch the shoulder seams.

2. Trim the facing seam allowances more narrowly than the garment seam allowances to eliminate bulk. Seam finishes are unnecessary on the facing. Press the seams open. Clip off the corners of the seam allowances at the neckline edges of both the garment and facing.

3. In order to minimize bulk, finish the outer edge of the facing by stitching and pinking. In unlined garments where the facing will show, finish with an edge stitch.

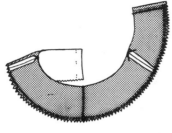

Steps 1-3

Joining the facing to the garment:

1. Pin and baste the facing to the garment, with the neck edges right sides together. Match the center front and shoulder seams. Fold the center back of the facing according to the type of zipper to be inserted.

If a lapped or welt placket zipper will be used:

(a) Fold back the facing on the left side ⅜ inch from the center back thread tracing. Fold the garment seam allowance along the center back thread tracing over the facing.

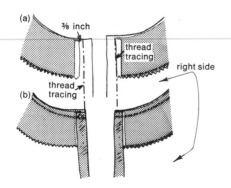

(b) Turn back the facing on the right side along the center back thread tracing. The seam allowance area on the right side of the garment will form an extension on the grain ⅛ inch beyond the center back thread tracing; this extension, which will conceal the zipper, is also turned over the facing.

For a slot or centered zipper:

(a) Fold back the facing ¼ inch from the center back thread tracing on both halves of the garment.

(b) Fold the garment seam allowance along the center back thread tracing over the facing.

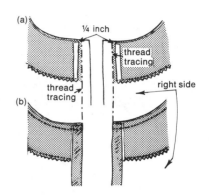

For an invisible or concealed zipper:

(a) Insert zipper before attaching the facing. Then fold back the facing on both halves of the garment ⅛ inch from the center back thread tracing.

(b) Fold the garment seam allowance over the facing along the center back thread tracing. The zipper is also folded over at this point.

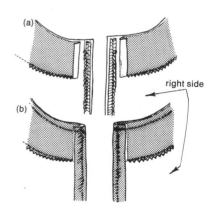

2. Stitch along the neckline on the garment side adjacent to the staystitching.

3. To prevent a ridge from showing on the right side of the garment, trim the seam allowance in layers. Trim the interfacing close to the stitches, the garment to ¼ inch, and the facing to ⅛ inch.

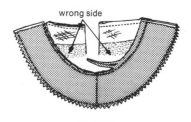

Steps 2-4

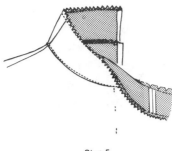

Step 5

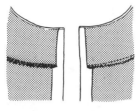

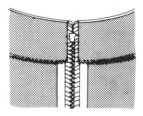

Step 8

4. To reduce puckers and allow the facing to lie flat around the neckline, clip the seam at ½ inch intervals close to the seam line. Clip the corners diagonally. In sheer fabrics, clip the garment and facing seam allowances alternately.

5. For casual wear and sportswear, back stitching is used to hold the facing to the inside of the garment. With the facing turned over the seam allowance, and the garment flat, edge stitch on the right side of the facing, catching the seam allowance.

6. For a couture finish at the neck edge, and to prevent the seam line from showing, roll the edge between your thumb and forefinger so the seam line lies slightly to the inside of the facing. Uneven basting ⅜ inch from the edge is optional, but must be removed before pressing.

7. Press the facing over the tailor's ham or press mitt, using a press cloth.

8. After the zipper is inserted, sew the facing to the zipper tape with small hem stitches.

9. At the shoulder seam, fold back the edge of the facing, and tack 1 inch from the neckline.

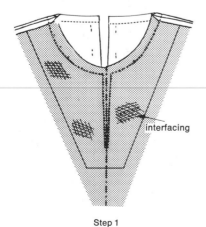

interfacing

Step 1

SLASHED NECKLINE AND FACING

1. To reinforce the slash, set the machine at 18 to 24 stitches per inch. Staystitch along the neckline seam to within ⅛ inch of the center thread tracing; with the needle down, pivot at the corner and stitch, tapering to the point. Take one or two stitches across the point and continue stitching the remainder of the neckline.

2. Pin and baste the facing to the garment, right sides together. Stitch on top of, or adjacent to, the staystitch.

3. Trim and clip the neckline. Cut carefully through the center to the point. Clip the corners diagonally.

4. Turn the facing to the wrong side. Pull out the corners and roll the edge of the garment so that the entire neckline and slash seam lies to the inside. Press.

When using a contrasting facing that will open toward the right side, the seam line of the slash should be rolled toward the right side of the garment and pressed.

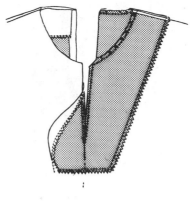

Steps 2-4

Square and V Neckline and Facing

1. To reinforce the corners or the V on the garment, set the machine at 15 stitches per inch and staystitch.

2. Pin, baste, and stitch the facing to the garment, right sides together. Stitch on the garment side to the corner or V; hold the needle in the fabric; take 1 stitch across the corner; pivot; and continue to stitch.

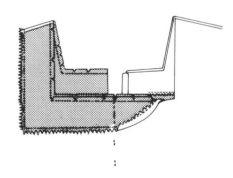

3. Trim and clip the seam allowance into the corner as close to the stitching line as possible. (Be aware that loosely woven fabrics ravel easily.) Continue to clip at regular intervals to relieve the tension in the seam allowance.

4. Turn to the right side and finish with back stitching; or press lightly, rolling the seam toward the inside.

Armhole Facing

Complete the shoulder and underarm seams of the garment.

1. Stitch the shoulder and underarm seam of the facing. Finish the outer edge with an edge stitch or with stitching and pinking. Trim facing seams more narrowly than those of the garment.

2. Pin and baste the facing to the garment, right sides together, matching shoulders, crossmarks, and underarm seams.

3. Stitch, trim, and clip.

4. As for a neckline facing, back stitch or roll the edge to the wrong side.

5. Press the facing over a tailor's ham or mitt. Turn back the edge of the facing ½ inch at the shoulder and underarm seam, and tack.

right side

Steps 1-3

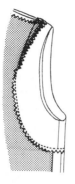

Steps 4 & 5

Neck and Armhole Combination Facing

The neck and armhole facing is used where the shoulder is narrow, because a combination facing is less bulky. To insure smooth edges and flat seams, attach interfacing to the garment and staystitch the garment.

1. Complete the garment and facing, joining shoulder and underarm seams. Trim the facing seam allowances more narrowly than those of the garment. Finish the outer edge of the facing with stitching and pinking.

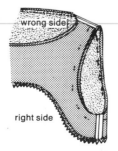

wrong side

right side

Steps 1 & 2

2. Pin and baste the facing to the garment, with the neck edges right sides together, matching the shoulders. Stitch, trim, and clip.

3. Back stitch the facing to the seam allowance, or roll the edge of the neckline to the inside of the garment and press.

4. Trim the armhole seam allowance of the facing and the garment to ¼ inch to allow flexibility in stitching the armholes accurately.

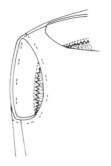

Steps 3 & 4

5. To complete the armhole, turn the garment to the right side. Position the facing on the garment, right sides together, and turn under the seam allowance of the garment to match the facing seam allowance.

6. With accurate seam allowances, basting is not necessary. Start stitching from the shoulder seam to the underarm and continue around to the other side of the shoulder. Gently pull the garment through as you are stitching, and clip at regular intervals to relieve the tension in the seam allowance. With a very narrow shoulder, it may be impossible to stitch the entire armhole by machine.

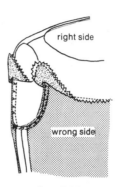

right side

wrong side

Steps 5 & 6

7. With a very narrow shoulder, slip stitch the facing to the garment where the shoulder has been left open.

8. Back stitch or roll the edge of the armhole facing to the inside of the garment and press.

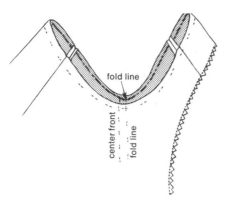

fold line

center front

fold line

Step 1

Self-Facing

Self-facing is used to eliminate a bulky seam on the front of jackets, shirts, or blouses; the center edge is cut on the straight grain and and the facing is cut in one with the garment.

The use of press-on interfacing eliminates the need for stitching at the center of the garment. With regular interfacing, catch stitch the interfacing to the garment so that the stitches are invisible on the right side.

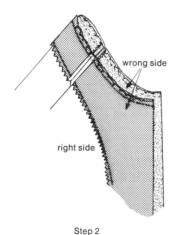

wrong side

right side

Step 2

1. Join the back neck facing at the shoulders, and finish the outer edge appropriately for the type of fabric and garment style.

2. Fold the facing back over the fold line and pin, baste, and stitch, right sides together, at the neck edge.

3. Trim and clip the neckline seam allowance and turn the facing to the wrong side.

4. At the hem edge, gradually shorten the facing to make it ¼ inch shorter than the garment at the outer edge. Trim heavy fabrics in layers in the hem area.

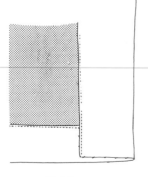

Step 4

5. Slip stitch the facing to the garment.

SHIRTBANDS

The shirtband—the strip on the right shirt front in which the buttonholes are made—eliminates the need for a facing. An extended self-facing is used on the left front. The shirtband is finished 1½ inches wide, but construction techniques vary, depending on the fabric and style of the shirt. Both the inside of the band and the left front are interfaced.

Shirtband Cut on Lengthwise, Crosswise, or Bias Grain, Single Width

1. Join the right side of the band to the wrong side of the garment at the raw edge.

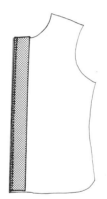

Step 1

2. Baste and stitch. Press the seam allowance toward the inside of the band.

3. Fold the band to the front, rolling the seam edge to the wrong side. Turn under the raw edge ½ inch, and top stitch ¼ inch away from the folded edge. To finish the band, top stitch the edge of the shirt.

Steps 2 & 3

Shirtband Cut on Lengthwise, Crosswise, or Bias Grain, Double Width

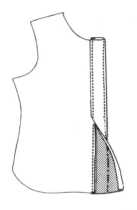

1. Attach the right side of the band to the wrong side of the garment at the raw edge.

2. After stitching, press the seam allowance toward the inside of the band.

3. Fold the band in half and turn it to the front. Turn under the raw edge, covering the seam, and top stitch through all thicknesses.

4. To finish, top stitch the edge of the shirt.

Shirtband Cut in One Piece with the Shirt

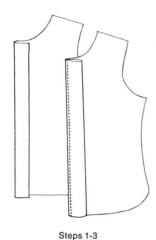

Steps 1-3

1. Turn the extension of the band 1¾ inch to the wrong side.

2. To encase the raw edge, fold over again.

3. Stitch ¼ inch away from this folded edge, which now becomes a French fold.

4. Stitch ¼ inch from the edge of the shirt.

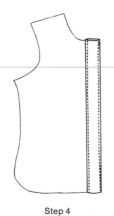

Step 4

Shirtband with a Loose Facing

1. Finish the outer edge of the facing appropriately for the fabric and garment style. Thread trace the fold line of the shirtband.

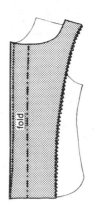

2. Join the band and garment, right sides together.

Steps 1 & 2

3. Press the seam allowance toward the inside of the band.

4. Turn the facing under along the fold line of the shirtband.

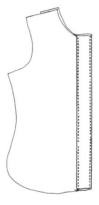

5. A convertible collar may be used with this shirtband. Insert the collar before top stitching ¼ inch away from the fold around the entire garment and collar.

6. Top stitch ¼ inch from the seam line on the band.

Steps 4-6

NECKLINE PLACKETS

Inserted Neckline Placket

An inserted neckline placket construction leaves a raw edge on the inside of the garment and is therefore used on garments that are worn closed.

1. Staystitch the squared opening.

2. Apply interfacing to the face of the plackets, and fold the plackets wrong sides together. Press lightly.

3. Join the garment and placket, right sides together, matching the raw edges. Stitch to the corners and tack.

4. Slash into the corners.

5. Align the placket right over left, and tuck the seam allowance at the bottom of the opening inside the garment.

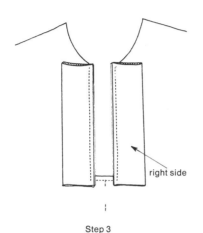

right side

Step 3

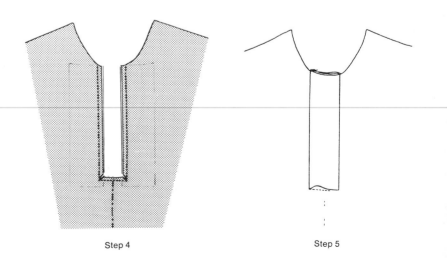

Step 4

Step 5

6. Turn the garment back to expose the seam allowance over the placket ends.

7. Stitch across, attaching the seam allowance to the placket.

8. Press.

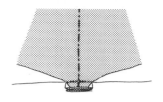

Steps 6 & 7

Inserted Neckline Placket with a Loose Facing

A faced neckline placket construction has a clean finish and permits the garment to be worn open.

1. Staystitch the squared opening.

2. Apply lightweight interfacing to the entire placket and thread trace the centers and fold lines on both placket pieces.

3. Finish the outer edge of the placket facings.

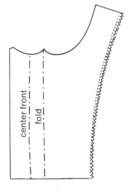

Steps 2 & 3

4. Join the garment and placket pieces, right sides together, matching the raw edges.

5. Stitch to the corners and tack.

6. Slash into the corners.

7. Turn the plackets at the fold lines and align right over left. Tuck the seam allowance at the bottom of the opening inside the garment.

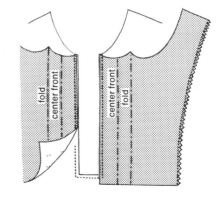

Steps 4 & 5

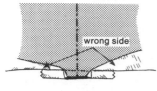

Step 8

8. Turn the garment back to expose the seam allowance over the placket and facings. Stitch across, attaching the seam allowance to the placket and facings.

9. Press the seam allowance into the placket and bring the facings to the neckline or shoulder seam.

10. The collar may be attached at this time.

Inserted Neckline Placket with a Pointed Tab

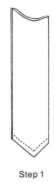

Step 1

The pointed tab placket is a variation of the inserted neckline placket.

1. Apply interfacing to both plackets.

2. Fold the right placket, right sides together, and stitch the pointed tab area.

3. Clip and trim the seam and turn the placket to the right side.

4. Press.

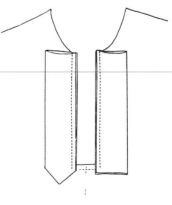

Step 4

5. Follow the directions for inserting a neckline placket (steps 3-6) applying the pointed placket to the right side of the opening.

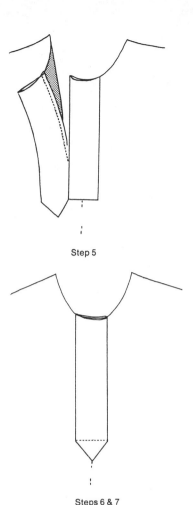

Step 5

6. Insert the left placket only into the base of the opening. Then continue with steps 7 and 8 of the same directions.

7. Pin the right pointed tab over the left, leaving the bottom of the tab loose.

8. Stitch across to secure the bottom of the tab, or top stitch to hold the entire point in place.

Steps 6 & 7

COLLARS

Collars are a design feature that enhances the appearance of a garment. There are standing, flat, and rolled collars in varying shapes and styles; examples include the mandarin, band, tie, convertible, shawl, shirt, sailor, and Peter Pan.

Collars may be cut in one piece with the outer edge on the fold, as a mandarin or

convertible. For a two-piece collar, the under collar is cut smaller so that the collar will lie smoothly and the outer seam edge will not be visible.

Collars are interfaced to support their roll and maintain their shape. The weight of the interfacing depends upon the fabric, the type of collar, and the final appearance desired. Interfacing is cut on the same grain as the under collar. Interfacing is applied to the under collar to prevent the seam allowance from showing on the right side of the finished garment. A lightweight backing may be applied to the upper collar. Press-on interfacing eliminates stitching the interfacing to the under collar.

Preparing the Collar

CONVERTIBLE, SAILOR, AND PETER PAN COLLARS

1. Apply interfacing to the under collar, clipping off the points of interfacings in pointed collars.

2. Thread trace the neckline seams of each section.

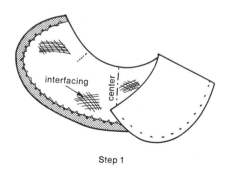

Step 1

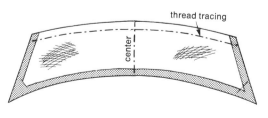

Step 2

3. Pin right sides together, matching the outer edges of the upper and under collars. Stretch the smaller under collar to fit it to the upper collar.

4. Baste along the outer edge close to the seam line.

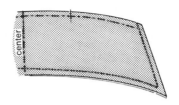

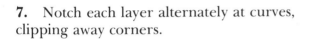

Steps 3-5

5. With the under collar facing up, stitch the outer edge. For collars with points, take one stitch across at the point and continue to stitch around the collar.

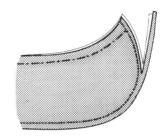

6. To reduce the bulk of the seam allowance at the outer edge, trim in layers, leaving the seam of the upper collar the widest.

Step 6

7. Notch each layer alternately at curves, clipping away corners.

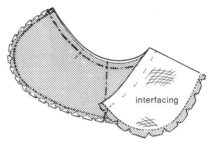

interfacing

8. Press the seam open, using the point presser at the corners and the press board at the outer edge.

Step 7

9. Turn the collar to the right side and roll the seam with the thumb and forefinger to the underside. Uneven baste along the edge.

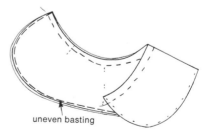

10. Baste the upper and under collars together along the neckline seam.

uneven basting

Steps 9 & 10

11. Remove uneven basting before the final pressing. Press lightly on the underside of the collar.

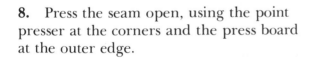

12. If the collar is to be made in separate sections, baste the two pieces of the collar together at the center front to insure their proper alignment in joining them to the garment.

MANDARIN AND BAND COLLARS

1. Apply interfacing to the outer collar.

2. Thread trace the neckline seam of each section.

3. Pin and baste along the outer edge and follow the directions for the convertible, sailor, and Peter Pan collars to stitch, trim, and press.

TIE COLLAR

1. Apply interfacing to the inner collar, excluding the ties.

2. Thread trace the neckline seam of each section.

3. Pin, baste, and stitch along the outer edge of the collar and around the ties to the neckline intersection, and tack.

4. Trim and clip into the intersection of the neckline; turn to the right side.

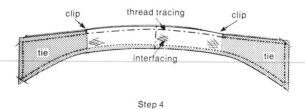

Step 4

5. Press the ties, rolling the seams to the edge. Press the collar, following the directions for the convertible, sailor, and Peter Pan collars.

COLLAR WITH ATTACHED TIES

1. Apply interfacing to the outer collar.

2. Thread trace the neckline seam of the collar.

3. Prepare the ties by hemming the raw edges.

4. Gather the ties to fit the ends of the collar.

5. Pin, baste, and stitch the collar, right sides together, with the ties inserted at each end.

6. Turn the collar to the right side and press, following the directions for the convertible, sailor, and Peter Pan collars.

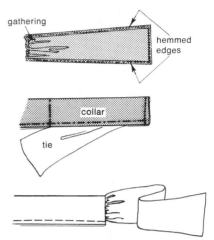

Attaching the Collar

JOINING A COLLAR TO A NECKLINE WITH A SHAPED FACING

1. With the upper collar facing outward, place the collar against the right side of the garment, matching the crossmarks at the center front, shoulders, and center back. Pin and baste, following the stay stitching on the garment neckline. A split collar may overlap in the seam allowance area at the center front.

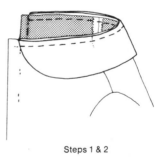

Steps 1 & 2

2. Join the shoulder seams of the facing. Trim the seams narrowly and press them open.

3. Finish the outer edge of the facing appropriately for the type of fabric and garment style.

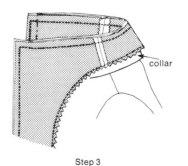

Step 3

105

4. Place the facing against the neckline, right sides together, sandwiching the collar, matching crossmarks, and allowing for zipper placement if necessary. Baste and stitch on the garment side.

5. Clip and trim the seam allowance in layers.

Joining a Collar to a Neckline without a Back Facing

1. With the upper collar facing outward, place the collar on the right side of the garment, matching the crossmarks at the center front, shoulders, and center back.

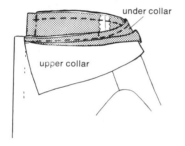

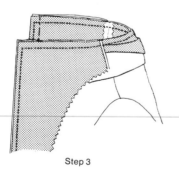

Step 2

2. Pin and baste, following the garment staystitching to the shoulder seam. Clip into the upper collar seam allowance and baste the under collar to the back neckline.

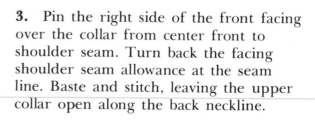

Step 3

3. Pin the right side of the front facing over the collar from center front to shoulder seam. Turn back the facing shoulder seam allowance at the seam line. Baste and stitch, leaving the upper collar open along the back neckline.

4. Clip and trim the seam allowance in layers.

5. Turn the facing to the right side, putting the seam allowance of the back neckline inside the collar.

6. Turn under the raw edge of the upper collar to the seam line and finish with a hem stitch, picking up the machine stitches and hemming the facing to the shoulder seam allowance.

7. Use a press cloth to press the front facing and under collar.

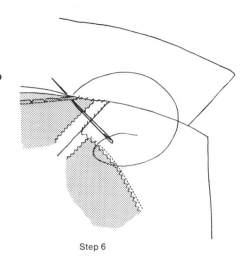

Step 6

Joining a Collar to a Neckline without a Facing

1. When a collar meets at the center of the shirtband or facing, the garment is cleanly finished to the center front. Join the band or facing, right sides together. Stitch from the outer edge to the center front. Clip to the stitching line at the center and turn to the right side.

2. Leaving the neckline seam of the collar open, place the outer mandarin, band collar, or under collar against the right side of the garment, matching crossmarks at the center front, shoulders, and center back.

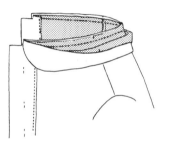

Steps 1-4

3. Pin and baste the single thickness of the collar, following the neckline stay stitching.

4. Stitch on the collar side. Clip and trim the seam in layers.

5. Turn the seam allowance into the collar and turn under the raw edge of the loose collar to the seamline.

6. Finish with a plain hem stitch, picking up the machine stitches.

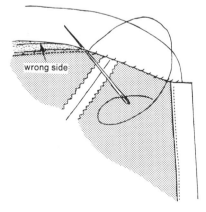

wrong side

Step 5

7. Use a press cloth to press the under collar.

Shirt Collar

1. Stitch the collar section in the same way as the convertible collar, finishing with a top stitch ¼ inch from the finished edge.

2. Apply the interfacing to the outer collar band section. The shirt band creates the stand for the collar.

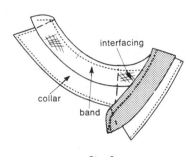

interfacing

collar

band

Step 3

3. Sandwich the collar, right sides together, between the top edges of the collar band, matching the center front crossmarks and the center back.

4. Baste along the seamline and stitch to the end of the band.

5. Trim the seam allowance to ¼ inch.

6. Clip, turn the collar band to the right side, uneven baste close to the seam line, and press.

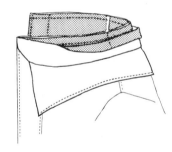

Step 7

7. To join the collar to the garment, pin the outer band to the neckline of the shirt, right sides together, matching the front extension, shoulder seams, and center back.

8. Baste and stitch along the neckline seam.

9. Trim and clip the seam.

10. Turn the seam allowance into the band, and turn under the raw edge of the inner band to the seam line. Hem, picking up the machine stitches.

11. To finish, on the right side of the band edge stitch close to the seam line along the neck edge to the collar intersection.

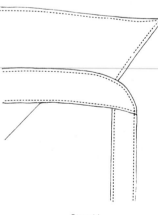

Step 11

12. Press lightly, using a press cloth on the inner band and under collar separately.

Shawl Collar

The shawl collar is cut in one piece with the front of the garment; an extended section rolls around to be joined to the back neckline. The upper collar also forms the front facing.

1. Apply the interfacing to the part of the garment front that includes the back collar.

2. Join the center back collar seams of the garment and facing separately.

3. Trim the seams in layers and press open.

4. To reinforce the shoulder and neckline intersection of both the garment and the facing, staystitch the corners.

5. Slash into the corners. Pin, joining the front and back shoulders of the garment and matching the intersecting seams at the neckline. Baste and stitch.

6. Pin, baste, and stitch the back under collar to the back neckline of the garment.

7. Clip and trim the neckline seam allowance and press shoulder and neckline seams open.

8. Finish the shoulder seams.

9. To complete the upper collar, insert the back neck facing, following the same procedure as for joining the back under collar to the garment.

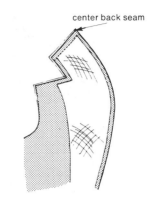

center back seam

Steps 1 & 2

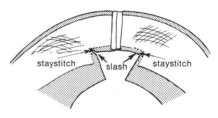

staystitch   slash   staystitch

Steps 4 & 5

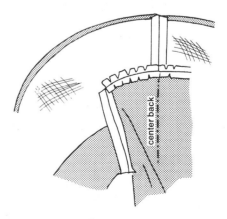

center back

Steps 5-7

109

10. Finish the outer edge of the facing.

11. Join the upper collar to the under collar, matching the outer edges. Baste, stitch, clip, and trim in layers. Press the seam allowance open, using proper pressing shapes.

12. Turn to the right side, rolling the seam line of the upper collar over the under collar and around the outer edge to the point where the facing rolls to the inside of the garment; then continue to roll the seam line into the garment. Uneven baste along the edge.

13. To hold the collar in place, slip stitch the seam allowance of the collar and facing together along the back neckline and shoulder seam.

14. Remove the basting before pressing. Press lightly on the facing and under collar.

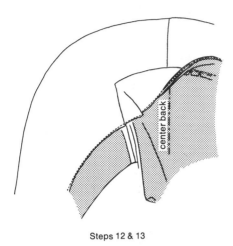

Steps 12 & 13

SLEEVES

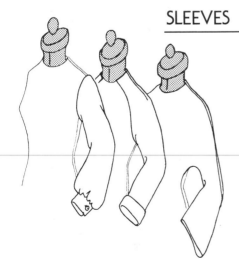

Sleeves fall into three categories: the mounted or set-in sleeve with a smooth or gathered cap; the semimounted sleeve, where the under half of the cap is fitted into an armhole; and the unmounted sleeve, where the sleeve is one with the waist of the garment.

Often the fabric used will decide the shape and style of the sleeve. The mounted sleeve, with or without a shortened cap, requires a fabric that can be molded or shrunk. When the fabric will not ease, and therefore will create puckers or pleats when the sleeve is set into the

armhole, another style should be selected—
the raglan, dolman, or semimounted
kimono sleeve.

To insure excellent fit and workmanship, the sleeve should be fitted into the
armhole on the dress form; basted, then
fitted on a model; and completed.

The Mounted or Set-in Sleeve

The armhole is usually the same for any
mounted sleeve; the shapes of the sleeve
and cap create the differences in style. In
mounting the sleeve, care should be taken
not to stretch the armhole. To mount a
smooth sleeve, steam shrink the fabric of
the upper half of the cap while keeping
the under half smooth, to maintain the
same grain as the bodice.

1.   In order to carry out both steps—
easing and maintaining the grain—make
an ease stitch around the entire cap from
underarm seam to underarm seam along
the seam line. One row of ease is sufficient to shape the sleeve, but for easier
handling a second row may be added ¼
inch away in the seam allowance area.

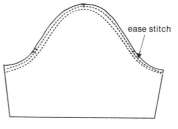

ease stitch

Step 1

2.   To shape the cap of the sleeve, pull
the bobbin thread at the center of the
cap, gently shaping the upper cap from
the front crossmark to the back
crossmark. The lower cap must be kept
smooth, with the ease stitching in this
area acting as a stay to prevent stretching. Pull the thread until the cap is
rounded out to the same dimensions as
the armhole of the garment. To eliminate puckers, distribute this ease evenly
between the crossmarks.

Step 2

111

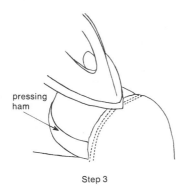

pressing
ham

Step 3

3. To set the ease, steam shrinking with the iron is essential. Place the upper cap face down over the pressing ham and gently shrink the ease. The end result will be a smoothly shaped cap without puckers. To insure that the cap has been eased sufficiently to fit the armhole, measure the armhole of the garment from front to back crossmarks and check this measurement against the sleeve. If additional easing is necessary, continue to pull up the ease and steam shrink.

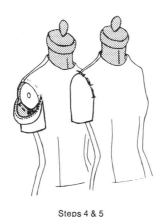

Steps 4 & 5

4. Before mounting the sleeve, complete the underarm seams of the sleeve and the garment and return the garment to the dress form. On the inside of the garment, match the underarm seam of the sleeve to the underarm seam of the garment and pin baste them together along the seam line, matching the crossmarks. Turn under the seam allowance of the molded cap and slip pin the upper cap to the upper armhole along the seam line.

5. Slip baste the sleeve into the armhole and fit it to the model. On the inside of the sleeve, stitch around the armhole.

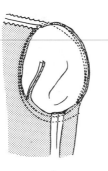

Step 6

6. To enlarge the armhole to a comfortable fit, stitch ¼ inch away from the seam line in the seam allowance area and trim the excess fabric close to the stitching.

7. Press the seams together on the inside of the sleeve, extending the tip of the iron ½ inch into the garment. The seam allowance should extend into the sleeve.

8. For a couture touch and to achieve a well-rounded look, a three-inch wide folded bias strip of cotton flannel is slip stitched between the crossmarks on the upper cap, along the seamline, trimming it to an elliptic shape in layers to eliminate a ridge on the right side.

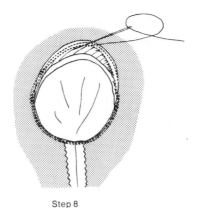

Step 8

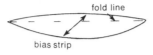

fold line

bias strip

The Puffed Sleeve

The puffed sleeve has additional fullness added to the cap and often to the lower edge. Two rows of gathering are necessary to pull up this extra fullnesss. The lower edge should be finished with a band, cuff, or bias before the sleeve is inserted into the armhole. Mount and finish the armhole in the same way as for the smooth cap sleeve, eliminating the steam shrinking.

The Semimounted Sleeve

The semimounted sleeve does not require easing or shirring to mount because the only area set into the armhole is the lower half of the sleeve, where the grains are balanced. The dress form is needed only to check the fit after basting, but not for the setting in of the sleeve. Whether the raglan, semimounted, or dropped shoulder sleeve is used, the underarm seam, overarm seam, or darts are stitched, pressed, and finished before the sleeve is joined to the garment.

THE SEMIMOUNTED KIMONO AND THE DROPPED SHOULDER SLEEVES

1. The semimounted kimono and dropped shoulder sleeves require staystitching of the corners of the garment and the sleeve. The seam is then slashed and opened to insert the sleeve.

2. With the right sides together, join the underarm seams of the semimounted kimono or the dropped shoulder sleeve. Stitch and finish the seam allowance.

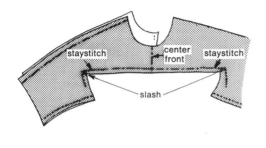

Step 1

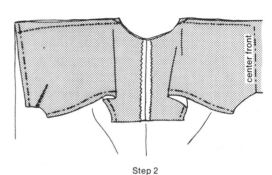

Step 2

3. Stitch and finish the side seams of the garment and the shoulder seam of the dropped shoulder.

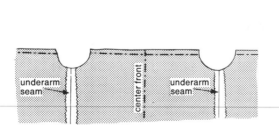

Step 3

4. The semimounted sleeve and the garment are joined right sides together along the style line by holding the slash point open. The dropped shoulder

114

sleeve should be eased slightly to fit into the armhole before joining to the garment. Pin, baste, fit, and stitch. Make a second row of stitching ¼ inch inside the seam line.

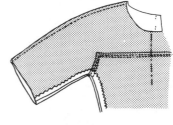

Step 4

5. Trim the seam allowance in the underarm area to the second row of stitching. The styled seam that joins the garment and the sleeve can be pressed together and trimmed.

6. Join the shoulder seam of the semi-mounted kimono.

THE RAGLAN SLEEVE. Join the raglan sleeve to the garment by following the crossmarks and matching the underarm seam. Stitch and trim the seam and press it toward the center of the sleeve or dart.

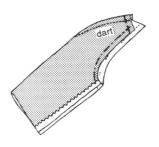

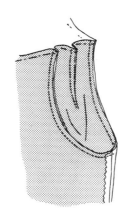

The Unmounted Sleeve

The dolman, kimono, and kimono with a gusset fall into the category of unmounted sleeves. The styling variations often depend upon the fabric used. The kimono with a gusset requires a firmly woven fabric that does not unravel.

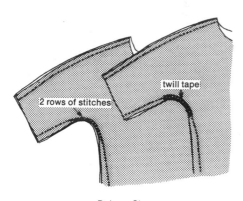

Dolman Sleeve

THE DOLMAN AND KIMONO SLEEVES

1. In the dolman sleeve, stress is often felt at the underam curve, where the seam is cut on the bias. When joining, reinforce this area of the seam with twill tape or two rows of stitches $1/32$ inch apart in order to prevent the threads from breaking.

2. To avoid puckering of the overarm seam, stretch the fabric slightly while stitching.

3. To allow the underarm seam to lie flat and to avoid pulls when the seam is pressed open, trim the seam allowance to $3/8$ inch in the curved area of greatest stress.

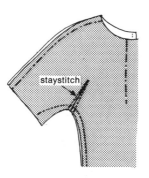

Step 1

THE KIMONO SLEEVE WITH GUSSET. To increase freedom of movement, which the dolman and kimono restrict, a gusset or diamond-shaped piece of fabric is inserted into a slash at the underarm. Often the gusset is divided lengthwise to form two triangles. Another version features an elongated gusset that becomes part of the lower sleeve.

1. To reinforce the slash line, staystitch along the seam line, taking one stitch across at the point. Cut along the slash line to the stay stitching.

2. Join the underarm and side seams, finishing the seam allowances and pressing open.

3. From the garment side at the underarm seam, with the right sides together, pin the gusset into the gusset opening, matching the intersecting points in the open slash. Baste.

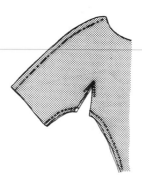

Step 3

116

4. Stitch from the raw edge of the gusset, crossing through the point of the slash to the intersecting seam of the garment. Leave the needle down at the seam intersection and pivot; then stitch through the opposite point to the edge of the gusset.

Repeat this procedure for the other half of the gusset. For ease in stitching, each side of the gusset may be stitched separately and the threads tied with the tailor's knot at the intersecting seams and points.

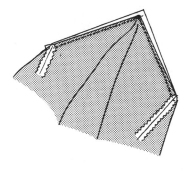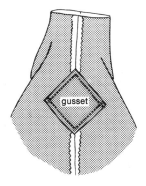

Step 4

5. The two-piece gusset is inserted before the seams are joined. After each half of the gusset in inserted, the underarm seam is stitched.

6. An option for further reinforcing the gusset is edge stitching the gusset along the seam on the right side of the garment.

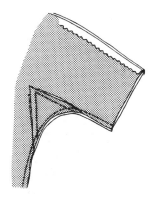

Step 5

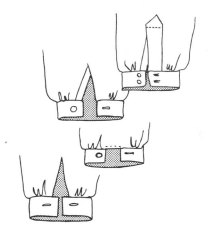

The finish at the end of the sleeve depends upon the style and shape of the sleeve and the garment. If the finish is in the form of a fitted cuff or band, an opening is made for the hand before the cuff is applied. This is an opening along the seam, a space between the ends of the cuff or band, a finished slash, a shirt placket, or a faced opening.

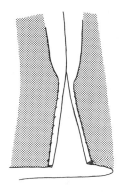

Seam Opening

Seam Opening

For an opening finished along the seam, stitch the sleeve seam, tacking at the point where the opening is to begin. To create a smooth finish, roll under the raw edge of the seam allowance and hem along the seam line. Press. Apply the desired cuff.

Hemmed Space

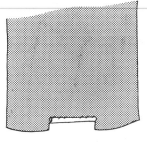

Hemmed Space

Allow sufficient space between the ends of the cuff or band for the hand; clip into the seam allowance; and hand roll or machine stitch this area. When applied and closed, the cuff or band will form a pleat in the space.

Continuously Bound Slash Opening

1. The bound slash calls for a strip of fabric 1¼ inch wide and twice the length of an opening 2½ to 3 inches. Either a lengthwise or a bias strip of fabric is appropriate.

2. After cutting the slash, open it so that it forms a straight line; align the edge of the strip along the slash, right sides together; and pin.

3. At the point of the slash, allow the seam on the garment to taper away from the strip, to permit a smooth and continuous seam. With a ¼ inch seam allowance, stitch on the garment side.

4. Bring the strip to the inside of the sleeve; turn under the raw edge ¼ inch and hem.

Covering the seam line ⅛ inch will make it possible to crack stitch the strip on the right side.

5. Turn the front of the strip against the sleeve opening, with the back strip forming an extension. When the strip is folded in this position, stitch along the fold at the top to hold it securely. Press and apply the desired cuff.

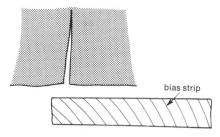

bias strip

Step 1

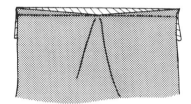

Steps 2 & 3

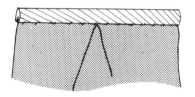

Step 4

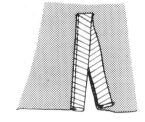

Step 5

Shirt Sleeve Placket

The tailored sleeve opening requires overlap and underlap pieces, which do not need interfacing unless the fabric is sheer.

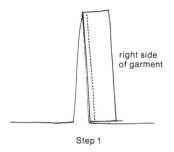

Step 1

1. Slash the opening and finish the back edge of the slash by placing the underlap face down on the inside of the back edge. Stitch, tapering to the top of the slash.

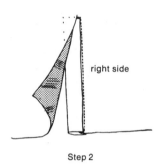

right side

Step 2

2. Turn the underlap to the outside. Turn under the raw edge ¼ inch and edge stitch.

3. Stitch the overlap face down to the inside of the front slash. Press the seam allowance and the strip toward the folded edge of the underlap.

Step 3

4. Turn the overlap to the outside along the fold; turn under the raw edges; and edge stitch. The top raw edge of the underlap is slipped under the overlap. Stitch across the overlap at this point to secure the placket.

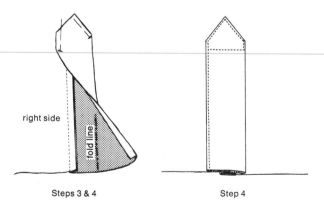

right side

fold line

Steps 3 & 4

Step 4

Faced Opening

The faced opening is rarely used in sheer fabrics.

1. Cut a piece of fabric the length of the opening plus 1 inch, and 2½ to 3 inches wide (with heavy fabrics, substitute a piece of lining). Finish the outer edge with an edge stitch.

2. Reinforce the slash by staystitching with the machine set at 18 to 24 stitches per inch. Taper to the point and take one or two stitches across the point.

3. Pin and baste the facing to the slash area, right sides together. Stitch on top of, or adjacent to, the staystitch.

4. Trim the seam and then cut the slash.

4. Turn the facing to the wrong side. Roll the edge of the slash so that the seam lies to the inside.

SLEEVE FINISHES AND CUFFS

Self-cuffs and Facings

TURN-UNDER HEM AND SELF-ROLLED CUFF

1. After joining the underarm seam, finish the hem edge with stitching and pinking or an edge stitch.

2. Turn under the hem to the width required for the hem of the turn-under hem or self-rolled cuff. Slip hem stitch or, for a sportswear finish, machine stitch. The stitching is concealed when the cuff is rolled.

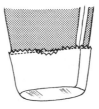

Hemmed Sleeve

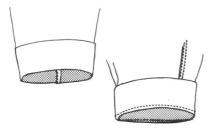

Step 1

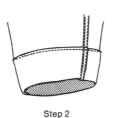

Step 2

SHORT SLEEVE SHIRT CUFF

1. After joining the underarm seam, turn under the hem to the width required for the cuff. Fold under the sleeve along this edge to encase the raw edge.

2. Pin, baste, and stitch ¼ inch away from the folded edge. Turn down the hem. The stitched fold forms the cuff on the right side of the sleeve.

CASING OR DRAWSTRING SLEEVE. A casing to enclose elastic or a drawstring is a suitable finish for a wider sleeve or a short puffed sleeve.

For elastic, turn under the amount needed to cover the elastic, plus a seam allowance. Turn the seam allowance under and edge stitch, leaving a 1-inch opening to slide the elastic through. Cut the elastic slightly shorter than the measurement of the wrist or arm, plus ½ inch for overlap. With a bodkin, tunnel the elastic; overlap the ends and stitch. Stitch the opening closed.

For a drawstring, turn under the amount needed to cover the drawstring, plus about ¼ inch for heading, and a seam allowance. Make a buttonhole in the tunnel area for the drawstring. On the wrong side, edge stitch the turned-under seam allowance. Leaving a tunnel ⅛ inch wider than the drawstring, make a heading by stitching a second row parallel to the first, near the finished edge. Thread the drawstring with a bodkin.

Separate Cuffs and Facings

Interface the face of the cuff, covering an area slightly wider than half the width of the cuff (to insure a smooth crease at the fold). With press-on or fusible interfacing, trim away all the seam allowance. With regular interfacing, catch stitch the edge near the center of the cuff.

BARREL CUFF. The barrel cuff finishes a gathered sleeve that does not have an opening. The cuff must be roomy enough to allow the hand to slip through comfortably.

1. Join the underarm seam of the sleeve, and gather the edge of the sleeve to fit the cuff.

2. Join the seams of the cuff and press open.

3. Pin, baste, and stitch the cuff to the sleeve, right sides together, adjusting the gathers and matching the underarm seams.

Step 3

4. Fold the cuff to the inside of the sleeve. Turn under the raw edge of the cuff and hem, picking up the machine stitches.

Step 4

SHAPED FACING WITH OR WITHOUT A CUFF. A shaped sleeve calls for a separate facing to finish the edge if more than a stitched or hand-rolled edge is desired. If a shaped cuff is used, it is sandwiched between the sleeve and the facing. A strip of bias may be substituted for a facing.

1. Join the seams of the facing and sleeve; trim the facing seams to ½ inch; and finish the outer edge.

2. Prepare a shaped cuff, cutting the under cuff slightly smaller than the upper cuff (the under cuff is interfaced). Pin the sections right sides together, matching the outer edges; stretch the under cuff to fit. Baste along the outer edge close to the seam line. With the under cuff facing up, stitch the outer edge. Trim the seam in layers, leaving the seam of the upper cuff the widest. Turn the cuff to the right side and roll the seam to the underside, uneven basting the edge. Baste the raw edges together. Press lightly on the underside of the cuff.

Step 2

3. Join the wrist edges of the sleeve and facing, right sides together, matching the underarm seams and sandwiching the cuff (take care to position the cuff so that the under cuff is against the sleeve). Stitch and trim in layers.

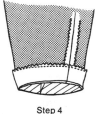

Step 3

4. Roll the seam, turning the facing to the inside of the sleeve. Hem the edge of the facing to the sleeve and press.

BAND AND FRENCH CUFF

1. To prepare the French and band cuff, fold right sides together and stitch and trim the ends. Turn to the right side, leaving open the edge that will be joined to the sleeve.

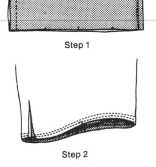

Step 4

Step 1

2. Join the underarm seams of the sleeve and gather or tuck the edge of the sleeve to fit the cuff.

Step 2

3. Pin and baste the open edge of the cuff to the sleeve, right sides together, matching crossmarks. If the sleeve opening is along the seam or is finished with a faced slash, allow for the lapped extension of the cuff. When attaching a French cuff, turn back both sides of the bound opening or finish with a faced slash. Stitch the cuff to the sleeve and turn the cuff to the inside.

For a cuff that is to be finished on the right side, join the cuff to the wrong side of the sleeve.

Step 3

4. Turn under the raw edge of the cuff and hand hem. Covering the seamline ⅛ inch will make it possible to crack stitch the cuff from the right side.

For a finish on the right side, turn under the raw edge of the cuff, cover the seam, and edge stitch.

Step 4

5. Mark and stitch the buttonholes. The buttonholes on a French cuff are made through both halves and each layer of the cuff to permit the use of cuff links.

ZIPPERS

The most widely used closure is the zipper. From the fine invisible to the bulky industrial, zippers can be both functional and decorative. The lengths vary from 4 to 24 inches. Zippers may be cut to any length, though longer zippers must usually be specially ordered.

Zippers with closed ends on woven tapes are the most widely used and are inserted by the lapped, slot, fly front, or exposed methods. Separating zippers are used in jackets or garments designed to be split and are inserted by the lapped, slot, or exposed methods. The most desirable for nonwaistline garments is the seam-like closure of the invisible zipper.

Casual or sportswear garment zippers are machine stitched; for a couture finish for dresses, skirts, or blouses, a hand pick stitch is suitable.

When the zipper opening is cut on the bias or in a knit, a stay of twill tape or a piece of china silk with the selvage attached should be hand stitched along the seam line of the opening on the wrong side of the garment.

Methods of Insertion

LAPPED OR WELT ZIPPER.   The lapped or welt application, most commonly found in skirts and at the back of dresses, is a popular technique to conceal the zipper.

1.   In order to conceal the zipper, an extension is needed along the back seam allowance. Form a tuck ⅛ inch beyond the seamline with pins. This tuck should continue for the entire length of the zipper tape. When inserting the zipper at the center back of the garment, the tuck extension is on the right back. For a side seam opening, the tuck is on the left back.

2.   Position the top of the zipper ¼ inch below the intersecting seam line, with the bottom stop even with the seam opening. Pin and baste the extended edge to the zipper tape. Line up this edge evenly along the zipper teeth to allow the slide to move freely.

3.   Using a zipper foot, machine edge stitch close to the folded edge to the end of the zipper tape.

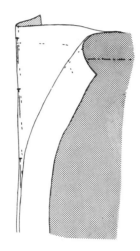

Step 1

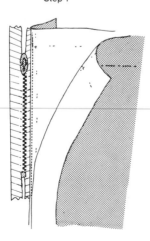

Steps 2 & 3

4. Fold the other side of the garment along the seam line. Pin this edge over the closed zipper, matching the folded edge to the thread tracing at the seam line on the other side.

5. To baste an even distance away from the edge of the fold and to allow room for the zipper slide to move freely, start at the top of the zipper and take a few small stitches to secure the zipper to the garment, and then open the zipper and continue basting. Slide the zipper closed to complete the basting, turning a right angle at the base of the zipper.

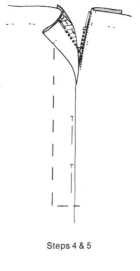

Steps 4 & 5

6. In order to machine stitch an equal distance away from the folded edge, follow the basting. Start stitching with the zipper open; then, holding the needle in the fabric, raise the presser foot and slide the zipper closed. Continue to follow the basting. For a clean finish, pull the thread at the base of the zipper to the wrong side of the garment and tie with a tailor's knot.

7. To hand finish, attach the overlap with a hand pick stitch. Then secure the zipper by machine stitching the seam allowance of the overlap to the zipper tape.

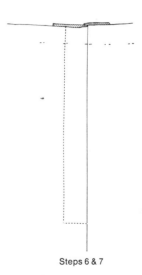

Steps 6 & 7

SLOT OR CENTERED ZIPPER. Another commonly used closure is the slot or centered zipper, suitable for skirts, blouses, and dresses.

1. Press both edges of the seam along the thread traced seam line.

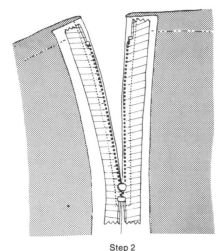

Step 2

2. Open the zipper and position the top ¼ inch below the intersecting seamline, with the bottom stop even with the seam opening. Pin the folded edge to just cover the zipper teeth. Baste an even distance away from the zipper to permit the slide to move freely and remain concealed when closed. When the zipper is closed there will be a slight overlap of the edges.

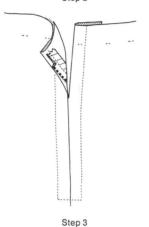

Step 3

3. To machine finish, stitch around the zipper with a zipper foot at an equal distance on each side, squaring off at the base of the opening.

4. To hand finish, attach the zipper with a hand pick stitch. Then secure the zipper by machine stitching the seam allowance to the zipper tape close to the hand stitching.

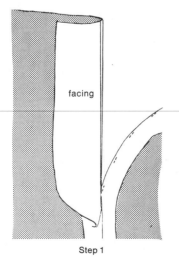

facing

Step 1

FLY FRONT ZIPPER. The fly front zipper is an important detail in women's slacks. A well-tailored look is achieved with a menswear-style application of the fly front zipper. Unlike most other zipper applications, the fly front requires both a separate facing and an underlay or fly shield. Use an eleven-inch trouser zipper with a special slide lock for fly insertions.

1. Face the left front opening, stitching, clipping, and trimming the seam to retain the shape.

2. To finish the right fly shield cleanly, stitch the curved edge, wrong sides together, and turn. Join the raw edges. The top of the shield is cleanly finished only if the slacks do not need a waistband.

3. In order to conceal the zipper, an extension is needed along the right front seam allowance. Form a tuck ¼ inch beyond the center tracing. Baste along the zipper teeth, allowing room for the slide and keeping the bottom stop level with the opening. The zipper may extend beyond the top edge of the slacks. Using a zipper foot, edge stitch the zipper in place along the full length of the tape.

4. On the right side of the garment, align the left front over the right front thread tracing and pin parallel to the edge.

5. Turn the garment to the inside and pin the zipper to the left front facing only. Baste and stitch the zipper to the facing, anchoring the tape with two rows of stitches.

6. On the outside, top stitch the zipper and facing to the slacks, following the thread traced stitching line. Draw the thread through at the bottom of the fly and tie with a tailor's knot.

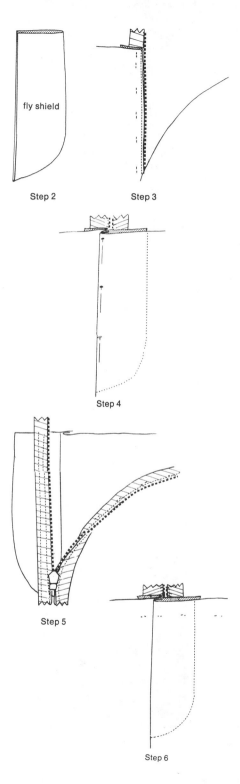

fly shield

Step 2   Step 3

Step 4

Step 5

Step 6

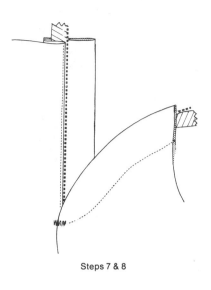

Steps 7 & 8

7. To insert the fly shield inside the slacks, line up the raw edges of the seam allowance and the fly shield, sandwiching the right front zipper tape between them. With the zipper foot, stitch along the raw edge and tack.

8. A bar tack will both reinforce the opening of the fly and keep the fly shield in place. The excess zipper may be cut away and the waistband may then be attached to the slacks.

EXPOSED ZIPPER. Exposed zippers of the nylon or polyester types are used in jerseys or sweater knits to give the closure flexibility, and the exposed industrial zipper, which has very pronounced metal or nylon teeth, adds another dimension to sportswear design. The exposed zipper is inserted into a slashed opening in the garment that does not call for a seam or facing. The neckline is finished after the zipper is inserted.

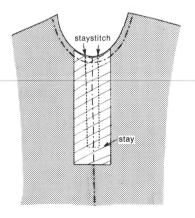

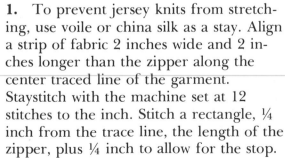

Step 1

1. To prevent jersey knits from stretching, use voile or china silk as a stay. Align a strip of fabric 2 inches wide and 2 inches longer than the zipper along the center traced line of the garment. Staystitch with the machine set at 12 stitches to the inch. Stitch a rectangle, ¼ inch from the trace line, the length of the zipper, plus ¼ inch to allow for the stop.

For the industrial zipper, prepare a wider opening (varying with the width of the zipper teeth) to allow the correct amount of zipper to show.

2. Place the zipper face down and upside down on the right side of the garment. The end of the zipper should be positioned clear of the stop. With a zipper foot stitch across the bottom, the width of the staystitching and tack.

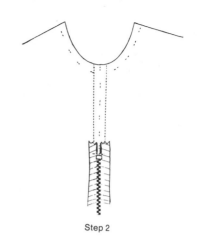

Step 2

3. To finish the zipper, cut the garment through the center to ¼ inch from the row of stitching at the bottom of the zipper, and cut diagonally into the corners. Turn the zipper toward the neck edge, with the stitched end tucked into the garment.

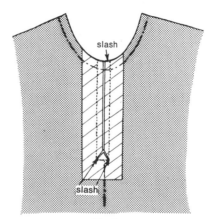

Step 3

4. On the inside, align the raw edge of the opening along the tape edge of the zipper and stitch, following the staystitching. For a closer finish, the opening may be stitched ⅛ inch from either side of the center tracing.

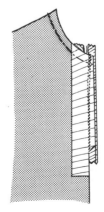

Step 4

Step 2

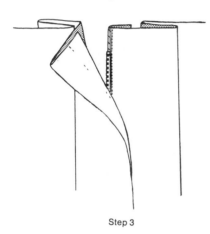

Step 3

ZIPPER IN THE SEAM OF A PLEATED SKIRT. In garments with all-around pleats, the zipper is inserted into the side seam. Proper positioning is important so that one pleat along the seam will completely conceal the zipper. The zipper is inserted into the seam, the final pleat is formed, and the zipper is finished on the pleat underfold.

1. Stitch the seam closed, allowing a sufficient opening for the zipper and a waistline seam allowance.

2. Clip the back seam allowance to the seam line, at the end of the stitching, and fold to the wrong side.

3. Baste the folded edge along the zipper teeth, allowing the slide to move freely, and stitch, using a zipper foot.

4. Open the zipper and place it face down over the front seam allowance with the zipper teeth ⅛ inch beyond the seam line. Baste and stitch along the zipper teeth and across at the zipper stop to the seam line.

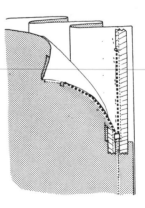

Step 4

5. Close the zipper and secure the pleats at the waistline. When top stitching the side pleat, stitch along the edge of the pleat to the base of the zipper and tack to the skirt.

6. Attach the waistband.

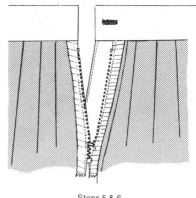

Steps 5 & 6

The Separating Zipper

The separating zipper is suitable for garments that are split. The lapped, slot, or exposed method is used.

For a front closing with a lapped or slot zipper, a finished hem and a full facing are necessary. The zipper is inserted between the garment and the facing.

1. Join the facing to the edge of the zipper tape. Fold the top edge of the zipper tape under and into the seam allowance. Stitch.

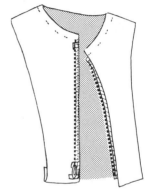

Step 1

2. Join the facing to the garment at the neck edge; stitch, trim, clip, and turn.

3. Complete the closure for the lapped or slot zipper.

For a front closing with an exposed zipper, a finished hem and a facing are also necessary.

1. Sandwich the zipper between the garment and the facing, allowing the teeth to show.

2. The tape of the zipper at both the top and the base is tucked under and into the seam allowance in order to cleanly finish the opening.

133

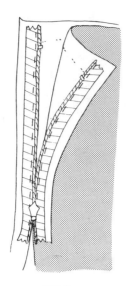

Step 2

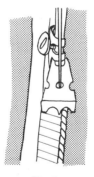

Step 3

The Invisible or Concealed Zipper

The invisible or concealed zipper's seam-like finish is frequently used for both front and back closures. This type of zipper seems to disappear in plaid or striped fabrics.

1. Close the seam, leaving the zipper length plus at least 3 inches open, or leave the entire seam open.

2. Press the zipper coils flat, adjusting the iron to a temperature that will not melt the zipper.

3. Place the open zipper face down on the right side of the garment with the edges of the tape parallel to the seam edges. Align the teeth of the zipper to cover the thread trace at the seam and baste each side close to the coils. Slide the zipper closed to check the alignment of the garment.

4. The use of a special foot designed for this zipper is necessary to sew close accurate stitches. Place the coil of the zipper under the zipper foot tunnels so that the needle will stitch along the sides of the coils, stitch to the slide and tack.

5. Use a cording foot to close the seam below the zipper.

WAISTBANDS

For a professional touch, the waistband selected to finish a skirt or slacks should give the garment a smooth, slim, and comfortable fit. Waistbands suitable to the style of the garment may be straight or contoured. To self-finish the waistline, an elastic or drawstring may be tunneled, giving the garment a close fit. For a clean finish, a facing of fabric, bias, or French grosgrain may be concealed inside the waistline.

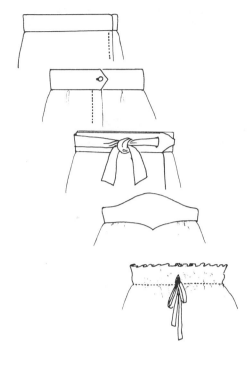

1. Waistbands are longer than the finished waistline to include overlap or underlap for buttonholes or hooks and eyes. The waistline of the garment is ¾ to 1 inch fuller than the finished waistline measurement. The extra fullness, which allows ease for a smooth fit, is accommodated when the garment is joined to the waistband.

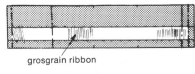

2. Always interface the waistband to give body and to prevent the waistline from stretching. Interface the inside of the face of a straight waistband, covering an area slightly wider than half the width. This will insure a smooth crease at the fold. If press-on or fusible interfacing is used, trim away all the seam allowance. If regular interfacing is used, catch stitch the edge of the interfacing close to the center of the waistband.

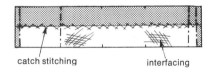

catch stitching   interfacing

To give a straight waistband a couture finish, interface with French grosgrain ribbon, determining the finished width of the ribbon by the width of the waistband. On the wrong side, catch stitch the ribbon inside the face of the waistband and along the crease line.

grosgrain ribbon

Step 2

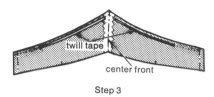

twill tape

center front

Step 3

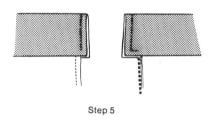

Step 4

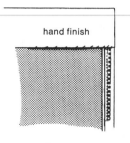

Step 5

hand finish

Step 7

3. On a contour waistband, in addition to interfacing the inside of the face, use twill tape to prevent stretching along the top edge. Before attaching the waistband to the garment, join the waistband pieces, right sides together. Stitch at the top edge, and then trim and turn.

4. With right sides together, join the waistband and the garment along the raw edges. Allow for the overlap or underlap to extend beyond the closure of the garment. Match the crossmarks to the seams, and adjust the ease of the waistline before basting and stitching. To reduce bulk, especially in heavy fabrics, trim the seam allowance of the garment after stitching.

5. To finish the ends of the waistband, fold right sides together on the crease line. When the waistband is to finish even with the edge of the opening, stitch from the folded edge to the waistline seam and tack. When the waistband forms an overlap or underlap, stitch from the folded edge to the waistline seam, turn the corner, stitch to the edge of the garment opening, and tack. Trim and clip. If the waistband is joined to tailored slacks, it will finish flush with the fly shield.

6. Turn the waistband to the right side. Press the ends and the fold. Turn the waistline seam allowance into the waistband.

7. For a couture finish, turn under the raw edge of the waistband and pin along the seam edge. Hem the edge, picking up the machine stitches.

136

8. For casual wear or sportswear, turn under the raw edge ¼ inch and edge stitch. The waistband will extend into the garment ¼ inch beyond the seam line. On the right side, crack stitch along the seam. Top stitching will give the waistband a crisp finish.

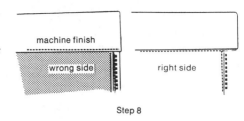

Step 8

9. To locate the position for the hooks and eyes or the button and buttonhole, close the zipper and overlap the waistband. The hooks and eyes are stitched in line with the zipper, hidden from view.

The Faced Waistline or Inside Waistband

A facing cut to the contours of the waistline of the garment gives a skirt or slacks an invisible waistband. Interface the waistband facing before it is applied.

FABRIC FACING. A fabric waistline facing is treated like a neckline facing.

RIBBON FACING. A couture method of treating a faced waistline is the use of French grosgrain ribbon, which is shaped with the iron to follow the contours of the garment.

1. To swirl the ribbon with the iron, shrink the waistline edge and stretch the edge that will remain free.

2. After shaping the ribbon, place the waistline edge of the grosgrain on the right side of the garment along the seam line, covering the seam allowance and allowing for the overlap or underlap. Fold under the ends of the ribbon and edge stitch to the waistline.

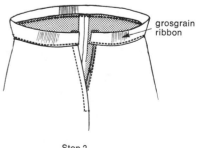

grosgrain ribbon

Step 2

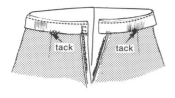

Step 3

3. To finish the waistline, turn the ribbon to the inside, rolling the edge slightly, and press. Tack securely at the seams and darts. A hook and eye will secure the ribbon inside the garment.

BIAS FACING. For a sportswear finish, use a double fold of interfaced bias as the waistline facing. Shape the bias with an iron and stitch, matching the raw edges, to the right side of the garment. Turn to the inside and tack at the seams and darts.

Elastic and Drawstring Waistlines

A self-waistband is used when the finish of the garment calls for an elastic or drawstring. The garment waistline may be the same width as the hip in order to eliminate an opening for a zipper or button.

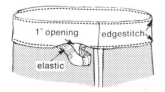

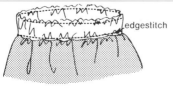

Step 1

1. For a self-casing for elastic, turn under the upper edge of the garment ¼ inch deeper than the width of the elastic, plus a seam allowance, to prepare a tunnel for the elastic. Edge stitch to the garment, leaving a 1-inch opening to slide the elastic through. Cut the elastic slightly shorter than the waistline measurement, plus ½ inch for overlap. With a bodkin, tunnel the elastic; overlap the ends and stitch together. Stitch the opening closed.

2. For a drawstring, a buttonhole will be needed on the face of the garment, and, in order to create a gathered effect, a heading is added. Fold over the desired amount, add ¼ to 1 inch for the heading, and then edge stitch. Stitch a second row parallel to the top edge for the heading, leaving the finished width of the tunnel ¼ inch wider than the drawstring. A closer, more comfortable, fit is achieved if elastic is substituted for the center back portion of the drawstring. Thread the drawstring through the buttonhole with a bodkin.

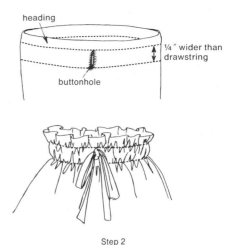

heading

¼" wider than drawstring

buttonhole

Step 2

Wrap-around Waistband

The wrap-around waistband with ties is attached along the entire waist of the skirt, with belt ties extending from each end. The tie slips through a buttonhole on the right front or left back to close the skirt.

For wrap skirts without belt ties, a hidden button is necessary to hold the underwrap in place. Another buttonhole on the outside closes the skirt.

ATTACHING THE WAISTBAND WITH TIES

1. Interface the skirt waistband.

2. Prepare the belt ties. For a single thickness tie, turn under the raw edge twice and edge stitch. For a double thickness tie, fold the fabric, right sides together, and stitch along the raw edges. Clip the corners, turn, and press.

3. Join the waistband to the skirt, leaving the ends open.

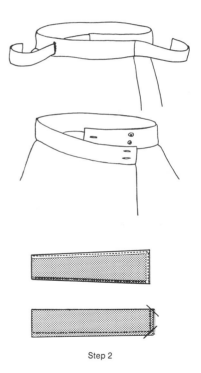

Step 2

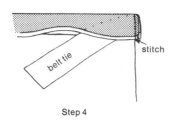

Step 4

4. Attach the belt ties at each end and stitch the ends closed.

stitch

belt tie

5. Complete the waistband.

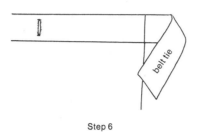

Step 6

belt tie

6. Stitch a vertical buttonhole on the right front or the left back to draw the tie through.

HEMS

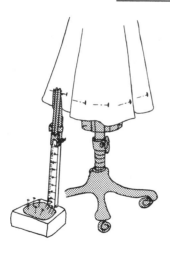

A hem is the final finishing step in a garment. It should be inconspicuous, but the type of hem used depends on the fabric and style of the garment.

Marking the Hem

In flared or circular skirts, it is suggested that the garment hang at least 24 hours to allow for stretching of the bias.

With the garment on the dress form or model, mark the hem with a pin marker or yardstick, placing the pins 2 to 3 inches apart. Accurate marking insures a professionally finished hem. Pin up the hem, and return the garment to the dress form to check for proper length. Turn up the hem seam allowance and uneven baste ½ inch from the folded edge on the wrong side. Trim the hem seam allowance evenly.

There are three different types of hems: straight, flared, and circular. The hem depth depends on the contour of the skirt and the fabric. The straight hem has no ease, and its depth can vary from 2 to 5 inches, according to the type of fabric: in sheer fabrics a deep hem adds a pleasing shadow and allows the garment to hang gracefully.

An A-line or flared skirt requires an eased hem to control the excess fullness; depending on the circumference of the skirt, 1½ to 2 inches may be turned up. The circular skirt requires a narrower hem because of its fullness; use 1 inch if the fabric shrinks easily, and less if it does not.

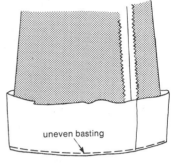

uneven basting

Circular Hem

1. To prepare excess fullness for shrinking in an A-line, flared, or circular skirt, ease stitch ¼ inch away from the raw edge, with the bobbin thread appearing on the right side.

2. Draw up the bobbin thread and distribute the fullness evenly, matching the seams without distorting the grain lines. To hold the ease in place, use either a staystitch or seam tape.

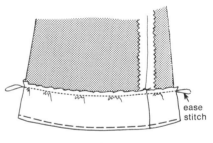

ease stitch

Steps 1 & 2

3. To shrink out the fullness, use a piece of heavy paper or poster board between the hem seam allowance and the garment. Holding the iron ½ inch away from the fabric, apply steam and shrink the excess fullness from the folded edge toward the ease stitch.

4. Complete the hem, using the correct hem finish.

5. Before pressing, remove all tracings and bastings. To minimize the crease and prevent the hem stitches from showing on the right side, press lightly on the wrong side and avoid the edge.

Seam Binding Hem Finish

Seam binding is used on hems to hide the raw edges of fabrics that unravel.

1. After the hem has been measured and turned up, stitch the seam binding along its edge, covering ¼ inch of the raw edge of the hem. Allow the binding to lay smoothly: do not pull or ease while stitching.

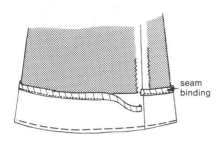

seam binding

2. When applying seam binding to circular hems, the tape can be shaped with the iron to follow its contours by stretching one edge and shrinking the edge that will be hemmed to the garment.

3. To finish, overlap ½ inch and then turn under the end of the seam binding.

4. Complete the hem, using the correct hem stitch.

Machine Hem Finishes

SINGLE STITCHED HEM. The edge stitch is a fine hem finish for sheer fabrics.

1. After the hem has been measured, trim away the excess seam allowance to ½ inch.

2. If the fabric stretches to an unusual extent, staystitch on the hemline before edge stitching.

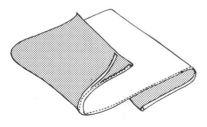

Single Stitched Hem

3. Turn under the ½ inch seam allowance and edge stitch.

4. Trim away the excess fabric close to the stitching line.

5. For silk and sheer cotton fabrics, an additional step for hiding the machine stitches is turning the hem edge to the wrong side close to the stitching and pressing with the iron at the correct temperature.

DOUBLE HEM STITCH. The double hem stitch is a casual or sportswear hem finish that gives a smooth and flexible edge to lightweight firmly woven and knit fabrics.

1. After the hem has been measured, trim away the excess fabric, leaving a ½ inch seam allowance.

2. Turn under the ½ inch seam allowance and edge stitch.

3. Stitch a second row ¼ inch away.

4. Trim away the excess fabric close to the stitching.

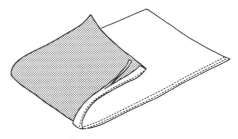

Double Stitched Hem

SHIRT HEM FINISH. The tailored shirt should be finished with a machine-stitched rolled edge following the contours of the bottom edge of the garment. The hemmer foot attachment turns and rolls the edge precisely, enabling the needle to catch the edge evenly.

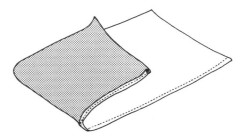

Rolled Machine Stitched Hem

BLOUSE HEM FINISH. To minimize bulk or a ridge showing through a skirt or slacks, a suitable finish for a blouse hem is a row of stitching and pinking at the edge of the garment. This secures the front facings and seams and prevents the fabric from unraveling.

Hems in Pleated Skirts

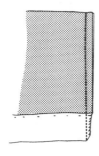

Step 1

1. On all-around commercially pleated skirts, the open seam is closed to the bottom hem edge, tacked, and trimmed diagonally, and the raw edge is overcast.

2. To finish the seam of a commercially pleated skirt in the hem area, remove the hemming to allow the seam to be joined flat. Complete the hem.

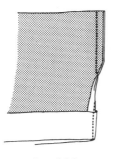

3. To hold the pleats in the hem area from opening, fold the pleat seam, right sides together, and bullet stitch along the inside seam.

Steps 2 & 3

4. A hem with fewer pleats can be treated like any other straight hem.

BUTTONHOLES

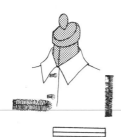

Buttonholes can be decorative as well as functional. The type of buttonhole used depends on the style and fabric of the garment. Bound buttonholes are made before the garment is assembled; hand-worked and machine-worked buttonholes are made after the garment is assembled. In-seam buttonholes are an opening along the seam. On women's garments, the buttonholes are made on the right front and left back and on the outer edge of skirt waistbands and cuffs.

The buttonhole should be ⅛ inch longer than the diameter of the button.

To determine the buttonhole size, tie a piece of paper around the button, or slash a cut in a piece of the fabric being used and slip the button through. The positioning and sizing of the buttonhole must be done with accuracy.

Bound Buttonhole

PLACEMENT AND MARKING.   Horizontal buttonholes are more secure on tight-fitting garments; vertical buttonholes are found on bands or loose-fitting garments. All markings are made on the interfacing and thread traced to the right side of the garment.

The average bound buttonhole is finished ¼ inch wide, but buttonholes on thin fabrics may be narrower and those on heavy fabrics wider.

1. Mark the center of the garment.

2. Mark the distance between the buttonholes along the center line.

3. Mark the length of the buttonhole. Horizontal buttonholes start ⅛ inch before the center line and finish toward the garment. Vertical buttonholes start ⅛ inch above the button placement on the center line (the ⅛ inch extra is to allow for the shank of the button).

4. Mark three lines for the width of the buttonhole: the center of the buttonhole and the marking on either side of the center should be twice the width of the corded strips.

PREPARING THE CORDED STRIPS

1. Buttonhole strips may be cut on lengthwise or bias grain and then corded.

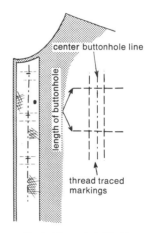

Vertical Buttonhole Marking

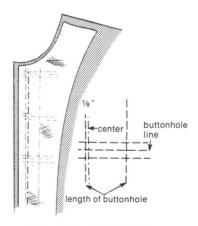

Horizontal Buttonhole Marking

145

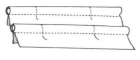

Preparing Corded Strips

2. Cut two strips for each buttonhole the length of the buttonhole plus 1 inch.

3. Thread trace the length of the buttonhole on each strip.

STITCHING

1. Pin the corded strips, aligning the edges at the top and bottom rows of thread tracing. Baste along the seam line of the cord.

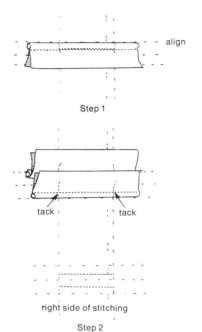

align

Step 1

tack   tack

right side of stitching

Step 2

2. Using the cording foot and 20 stitches per inch, stitch the length of each buttonhole, tacking at both ends. Check that the stitches are parallel on the wrong side.

3. Remove all thread tracings and bastings.

Step 4

4. Cut through the center of the garment and interfacing to within ⅜ inch of each end, and clip diagonally into each corner. On small buttonholes, cut diagonally from corner to corner.

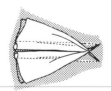

Step 5

5. Pull the strips to the wrong side and position them to meet at the center. Baste together closely.

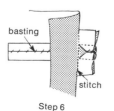

basting

stitch

Step 6

6. Fold the garment back, exposing the triangle. Center the strips, stitch, and tack the triangle to the corded strip.

7. Press lightly on the wrong side, using a piece of oaktag under the strip to prevent ridge marks on the right side.

FACING. Bound buttonhole finishing can be oval or rectangular. The oval is most commonly used, but for a more exacting buttonhole shape, and when finishing heavier fabrics use the rectangular method.

1. Join the facing to the garment.

2. Baste the facing around each buttonhole to prevent shifting.

For the oval finish:

1. Pin through the center of each end of the buttonhole from the right side through to the facing.

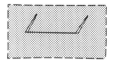

Steps 1 & 2

2. Slash the facing between the pins, extending the slash by a few threads on each side.

3. Turn under the raw edges and hem with small stitches, picking up the machine stitches of the buttonhole and reinforcing the ends.

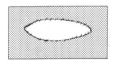

Step 3

For the rectangular method:

1. Pin through each corner of the buttonhole from the right side through the facing.

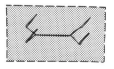

Steps 1 & 2

2. Slash through the center and to within ⅜ inch of each end, and then clip diagonally into each corner.

3. Turn under the raw edges and triangles. Hem with small stitches, picking up the machine stitches of the buttonhole.

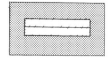

Step 3

In-seam Buttonhole

To prevent stretching when the inseam buttonhole is used, either interface the buttonhole or back or underline the entire garment. Place the interfacing into the seam allowance ⅛ inch past the seam line.

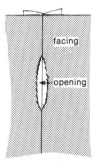

interfacing

1. Mark each end of the buttonhole opening with chalk.

2. Pin and baste the garment sections together.

3. Stitch and tack along the seams, interrupting the stitching for the buttonhole opening.

Inseam Facing

1. Finish the inseam facing the same as the facing of the bound buttonhole.

2. Slip stitch the opening of the buttonhole and the facing together.

In-Seam Facing

One-Piece Facing

1. Baste the facing around the buttonhole to prevent shifting.

2. Finish with either the oval or the rectangular method.

Hand-worked Buttonholes

Hand-worked buttonholes can be vertical or horizontal.

Vertical buttonholes are finished at both ends with bar tacks or fan stitching. Horizontal buttonholes have bar tacks at both ends or fan stitching at one end.

1. On the right side of the garment mark the width and length of the buttonhole.

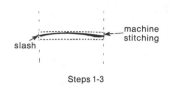

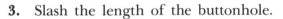

Steps 1-3

2. To prevent the fabric from unraveling and to hold the layers of the garment while stitching, machine stitch around the shape of the buttonhole, using 20 stitches per inch, $1/16$ inch from the marking.

3. Slash the length of the buttonhole.

4. With buttonhole twist, working from left to right, bring the needle to the right side just below the machine stitching, swing the thread around the needle and take another stitch close to the first one. This action forms a purl at the edge. Continue this stitch on one side of the buttonhole.

Step 4

5. To form a fan at the rounded end, fan 5 to 7 stitches at the same depth, keeping the purl in line with the opening. Turn and continue along the other side.

Step 5

6. For the bar tack, take several long stitches across the end of the buttonhole. Cover these stitches with the buttonhole stitch, keeping the purl to the inside. For a vertical buttonhole, finish both ends with bar tacks or both with fans.

Step 6

Machine-worked Buttonhole

Machine-worked buttonholes are made on the buttonhole machine. Many sample rooms do not have a buttonhole machine and, therefore, must send out the sample for buttonholes. Machine-worked buttonholes are marked with a pencil dot on the right side of the garment where the buttonhole is to start. The buttonhole machine will both stitch and cut the buttonhole.

Eyelets

Step 1

Step 2

1. Eyelets are made by hand or machine. The eyelet machine will cut and stitch the eyelet.

2. To make the eyelet by hand, punch a hole with an awl. Run a row of hand stitching around the hole and complete the opening with the buttonhole stitch.

BUTTONS, HOOKS AND EYES, SNAPS

Buttons

Buttons are an important trim or finish for a garment. There are two types, shank and sew-through, found in many different materials. The shank button permits the buttonhole fabric to close without puckering. The sew-through button needs a thread shank to equal the thickness of the fabric.

BUTTON PLACEMENT

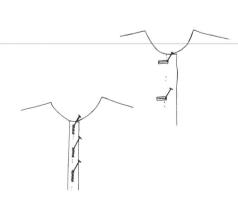

1. Overlap the centers of the garment with the finished buttonhole on top.

2. Pin horizontal buttonholes through at the centers and mark.

3. Pin vertical buttonholes ⅛ inch from the top of each buttonhole and mark.

STITCHING BUTTONS. To attach the buttons, use heavy-duty thread, doubled, or several strands of matching thread.

For garments that are to be worn closed, stitch through the garment and facing; for garments worn open, catch only the garment and interfacing.

To sew two- or four-hole buttons, secure the thread with a few small overcast stitches or an inconspicuous knot. Holding the button away from the fabric, come up and down through the holes in the button, allowing some slack in the thread, which will create a shank. To finish, secure the thread and bring the needle through to the right side behind the button, wind the thread tightly around the slackened thread that attaches the button; and end securely.

Two–
or Four–Hole
Buttons

To sew shank buttons:

1. Secure the thread with a few small overcast stitches or an inconspicuous knot.

2. Sew through the shank with an overcast stitch, ending securely.

3. When the shank button needs extra play, hold the button away from the garment slightly while overcasting. Then wind the thread around the added thread shank and end securely.

Shank Buttons

REINFORCING BUTTONS

1. On heavy garments, where there is a strain on the button, reinforce with a small button on the inside of the garment.

2. Sew through this button at the same time as the garment button, keeping the stitches in line from one to the other.

Reinforcing Buttons

Do not omit making a thread shank on the surface button.

Hooks and Eyes

Hooks and eyes are hidden fasteners used to secure waistband closures and neckline tops, where there may be a strain on the garment. Several hooks and eyes are necessary to secure waistbands. The number of hooks and eyes is determined by the width of the waistband. Trouser hooks may be substituted for a more secure closure on skirts or slacks. Eyes are made of metal or thread: the thread eye is less conspicious than the metal eye, but not as strong. A double thread is recommended for secure stitching to the garment.

1. Place the hook in position on the garment ⅛ inch from the edge on the underside of the overlap.

2. Catch the underside of the fabric only and overcast each loop of the hook. Slide the needle through the fabric to the end of the hook and overcast a few stitches to secure the head of the hook to the garment.

3. Overlap the garment and mark the position of the eye, using the head of the hook as a guide.

4. Center the metal edge over the dot and overcast the loops.

THREAD EYES. The thread eye, used as a substitute for the metal eye, is measured so that the head of the hook slips over it. Elongated thread eyes are used for button loops and belt carriers. The button loop is equal to the diameter of the button. The belt carriers are ¼ inch longer than the finished belt. There are two methods for forming these eyes, loops, and carriers: (1) making a chain; and (2) using the buttonhole stitch over a thread bar (the buttonhole method is stronger). For either type, use heavy-duty thread or buttonhole twist.

For the thread chain method:

1. Mark the length needed.

2. Secure the thread on one side and leave a loop to start.

3. Hold the needle thread securely in one hand and the loop in the other hand. Pull the needle thread through the loop to form another loop.

4. Tighten the loop to form a chain and continue this action until enough chain is completed.

5. To end the chain, pull the needle through the last loop and secure on the wrong side.

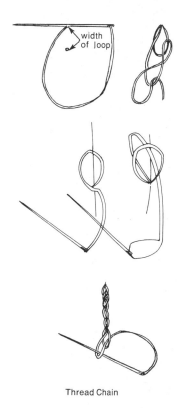

Thread Chain

For the buttonhole stitch method:

1. Mark the length needed.

2. Take three long stitches to form a bar.

3. Working from left to right, swing the needle thread over the bar to make the hand-worked buttonhole stitch.

4. Keep the stitches close together, covering the bar.

5. Finish securely on the wrong side.

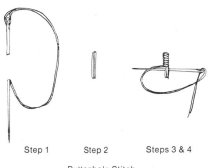

Step 1   Step 2   Steps 3 & 4

Buttonhole Stitch

153

Snaps

Snaps are invisible fasteners used when there is no great strain on the garment and an inconspicuous closing is needed. Snaps can be covered in thin fabric, color matched to the garment. The snap consists of a ball and socket.

1. Place the ball of the snap on the underside of the overlap away from the edge.

2. Catching one layer of fabric only, take several stitches in each hole to secure it to the garment.

3. Overlap the garment; mark the position of the socket on the other side of the garment, using the ball as a guide; and stitch. The socket can be stitched through to the underside of the garment for additional security.

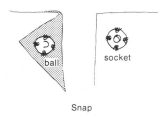

Snap

COVERING SNAPS

1. Cut two pieces of a lightweight fabric twice the diameter of the snap.

2. Make small running stitches around the edge of each piece.

3. Wrap the ball and socket (separately) in the fabric; the fabric should just meet and not overlap. Then gather up the fabric and stitch it securely at the rear of each piece.

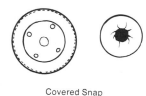

Covered Snap

4. Snap the ball and socket together to puncture the hole and expose the top of the ball.

Special Detailing

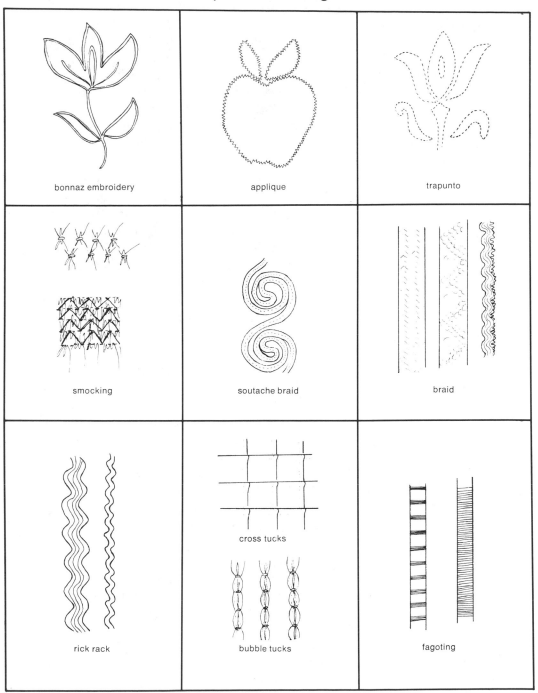

bonnaz embroidery

applique

trapunto

smocking

soutache braid

braid

rick rack

cross tucks

bubble tucks

fagoting

TRIMMINGS

The use of trims adds another dimension to a well-designed garment. The variety of trims is extensive, and with every season new trims are added to the already tremendous selection. Some trims are applied in the sample room, as they can be stitched with the single needle machine. For production, the application of trim is sent out to a contractor, because many types of trimmings require application by special machines. Trims that can be applied in the sample room are bindings, flat braid, ribbon, fringes, ruching and ruffles, rick rack, lace edging, and insertions.

To secure trim to the garment, stitch on either edge or through the center. Lace insertion is stitched along both edges and the fabric trimmed away underneath close to the machine stitching. If the fabric unravels, the raw edges are cleanly finished first, and then the lace is inserted. Edging or ruffled lace is sewn along a finished edge or sandwiched between two pieces of fabric.

Types of special detailing that are applied by the contractor using special machines include appliqués, beading, sequins, bonnaz embroidery, braids, crocheted edging, eyelets, fagoting, nailheads, quilting, smocking, soutache, trapunto, and tucking. In addition, there are specialists who do hand application of beading and embroidery.

Index